BY
WANKERS OF THE WORLD

WELBECK

THIS BOOK IS A PARODY!

DISCLAIMER

This book is in its entirety a satire and parody publication solely for humorous entertainment and editorial purposes, which uses actual names in quasi-real and/or fictitious narration. All articles, stories, competitions, games, news stories, illustrative materials (images and illustrations) contained within this book are **100% fiction and fake.**

Any resemblance to the truth is purely coincidental and accidental with no intent by the publisher for it to be a factual statement, except for all references to names of politicians, celebrities and/or other personalities that are named, critiqued and/or commented upon, in which case their name is based on real people, but is entirely fictitious and parodic.

The publisher makes no representations or warranties with respect to the accuracy or completeness of the contents of this book and specifically disclaim all warranties, including without limitation warranties of fitness, accuracy and factual representation for any particular purpose. No warranty may be created or extended by sales or promotional materials. This book is sold with the sole understanding that the entirety of the content is fictitious. The publisher shall not be liable for any damages arising herefrom.

Published in 2021 by Welbeck

An Imprint of Welbeck Non-Fiction Limited, part of Welbeck Publishing Group

20 Mortimer Street, London W1T 3JW

Design and Concept © 2021 Wankers of the World
Text © 2021 Welbeck Non-Fiction Limited, part of Welbeck Publishing Group

A CIP catalogue record for this book is available from the British Library

ISBN 978-1-80279-024-5

Printed in Slovenia

10 9 8 7 6 5 4 3 2 1

FSC
www.fsc.org

MIX
Paper from responsible sources
FSC® C106600

Win! Festival of Brexit Tea Towel **P18**

P8

Sneaky Peek

P12

Inside this edition...

P36

P4

P38

P42

P56

wankersoftheworld.com
@wankersoftheworld

Don't Miss

P7

P30

P59

P11

Win!
Test & Trace Contract!

£150 BILLION

FIND THE Money!

Are you childhood chums with people called Otto, Tarquin or Darius? If the answer is no then you probably haven't received a lucrative Test & Trace or PPE government contract. But don't worry! Have a Wank is offering one lucky reader the chance to win £150 billion worth of COVID trade!

LOOK FOR

- BlameNHS
- Contracts
- Excess
- Outsource
- Chumocracy
- Deaths
- Isolation
- PPE
- ClapNHS
- EtonMess
- Mortality
- Serco

N	Y	B	H	T	F	E	C	G	O	Z	S	E	R	C	O
I	K	D	L	S	V	J	A	O	W	H	Q	N	U	P	H
S	B	V	B	D	S	I	O	N	N	S	I	E	L	E	W
O	S	S	T	N	S	E	K	E	L	T	M	G	R	T	E
L	V	H	A	J	K	P	M	B	P	H	R	B	D	M	C
A	N	T	Z	Y	O	A	S	N	Y	P	T	A	C	O	R
T	P	A	S	C	L	H	S	G	O	R	Y	O	C	R	U
I	C	E	A	B	N	M	Z	R	N	T	D	S	E	T	O
O	O	D	W	P	N	E	A	P	H	C	E	K	V	A	S
N	L	S	A	S	S	E	C	X	E	O	N	A	J	L	T
A	G	L	T	O	K	Y	E	L	F	K	Y	K	T	I	U
W	C	H	U	M	O	C	R	A	C	Y	E	D	P	T	O
H	L	Y	V	A	T	Y	W	S	R	C	M	Z	C	Y	W

FINISHED? Call the competition hotline now!

0203 026 2491*

*Not a real competition

Love Dirty

Family man?

Starting a family with my man was a dream. Until I got a surprise kick in the teeth!

By Carrie, 33, from East Sheen

I tore open the envelope and pulled out the contents. What I saw in front of me changed everything. It was like I'd been hit by a steam train. Suddenly, all those worries that had been eating away at me for months made sense. How could I have been so stupid?

It had all seemed so different when I met Boris. It was just an ordinary Friday at the office: making tea and leaving passive-aggressive comments under my friends' Instagram posts.

Then, suddenly, he appeared. I'd never met anyone like him: he was like a big, posh albino Honey Monster. When he spoke my ovaries nearly exploded! He was all mumbled Latin phrases, historical names and racist jokes. I was, like, phwoar!

Someone asked him if he wanted a tea or coffee and he said he'd prefer an 'aqua vitae'. When we all looked blank he explained that this meant a glass of water. How clever! I said I'd get it and he barked: 'That's the spirit – carpe diem!' I didn't know what that meant but somehow it made me feel I could really trust him.

I'll be honest, I was pretty shocked when he paid me attention. Why was this bumbling, chubby, posh man interested in little old me? I toyed with my hair and played it cool by telling him about how tiny microplastics are poisoning our oceans but he stopped me mid-flow by placing his finger over my lips – well that's what he tried to do. In actual fact, it ended up halfway inside my mouth. I remember it tasting like Wotsits. But I'd got the message to stop talking. Then it happened: 'Shall we go for errm, would you care to err, dinner?' he asked. My heart began thumping so hard. Naturally, I said yes.

Rat's Dozen!

Eyes of a scumbag

Me with Boris

He took me to a really nice Harvester just off the A34 near Didcot. It was utterly romantic. He told me he was very rich but liked to be seen as a normal pint-swilling British bloke. As I gnawed the last morsels of meat off my BBQ glazed ribs, I sank back into my chair and smiled. I was so happy.

Suddenly, he got all fidgety and roared: 'Let's leave!' He clicked his fingers loudly in the air several times to attract the attention of the waiter, pointed at me and said: 'Can she get the bill, please?' That should have

been a red flag. Looking back, I can't remember him paying for a single drink or meal.

All the same, he invited himself back to my place and before long his chubby sausage-fingered hands were struggling with the buttons on my blouse.

After that wonderful first night, our relationship blossomed into a real fantasy romance. Even my dog Dilyn took a shine to him. He would often take off his shoes and let Dilyn hump his bare, sweaty feet. What a sweety!

But it wasn't long before the warning signs started flashing. I lost count of the number of times I caught him lying.

I felt something big wasn't right, but the more he pushed me away the more I'd make an effort. One night I cooked him his favourite meal – bangers, mash, pork chops, lamb's liver, chips, peas, roasties and chips. He promised to be home early but by 9pm he hadn't shown up. I phoned him in floods of tears but he just mumbled that he was in a meeting. In the background, I heard an American woman shouting: 'Alexander the Great, get back into bed this instant!' What did it mean? He was so cryptic.

I tried to talk to him but he hated confrontation and would say anything to avoid facing the truth. He also stopped caring about his appearance and point-blank refused to brush his hair or his teeth – which had become yellow and furry. Suddenly, my dishy dream had turned into a nasty nightmare.

But it was the day I asked him how many children he had that I began to see his true colours. He'd mentioned there might be 'one or two', but when I asked how many, he refused to answer. He would just shout: 'It's time to move on!' and 'The British public isn't interested in this tittle-tattle!'

Well, I was interested! One Sunday afternoon when he was grouse shooting with his friend Darius, I decided

He'd say anything to avoid the truth

to open up one of his bank statements. They were all piled up in a mess on the floor by the door, so I knew he wouldn't notice one missing. I tore open the envelope and let out a shriek – literally every other payment was a large sum going to CHILD SUPPORT. What a bombshell!

I checked his laptop next. It had a password but I guessed it right first time: ChurchillsBigCigar45. I knew him so well. Or so I thought, because what I discovered next made me sit bolt upright. He didn't just have 'one or two' children – he had 12! I felt mortified. As the tears filled my eyes I looked down at Dilyn. He looked so limp and flaccid. It was horrific.

From then on we would argue all the time. It got so bad one night that a neighbour called the police. I was mortified! People were telling me I could do better and should dump him, but Boris kept saying if I just hung on he would become a lord and then I would become the Queen. I didn't know much about the Royal Family, but who could resist that?

I decided to take the plunge and we've just had our first baby together. He told me he's so proud to be a father for the thirteenth time. We also got married and on our wedding day, he told me that 'he really loves me… being alongside him for a photo opportunity.' I'm feeling really positive about our future together.

My true love: Dilyn

THE MOST COMPLETE ANSWER TO NEEDLESS DEATH

TONY BLAIR
Walk-in Blood Bath

UP TO 90% MORTALITY

18 YEARS

"The best way to relax!"

Tony Blair

Tony Blair

- **PAIN & SUFFERING GUARANTEED!**
- **WAR CRIME RESISTANT COATING**
- **EASY TO INSTALL TROOPS**
- **EFFICIENT KILLING OF WOMEN & CHILDREN**
- **ONLY £29 BILLION SPREAD OVER 18 YEARS**

"Enjoy a guilt-free soak!"

MADE IN UK & USA

FOR YOUR WORRY-FREE BLOOD BATH JUST CALL
0203 026 2491

WOTW

WANKERSOFTHEWORLD.COM

Fashion Hacks

Want to look your best? Then check out these style ideas.

Boosted by boots!

Real-Life Reader Advice!

Are you worried about your height? Simon from Elstree writes in to tell us about a wonderful little life hack. 'Despite my high-powered job, I was always really insecure about being such a short little prick. I even caught myself bullying children to make me feel bigger. It was awful! But my life changed the day I bought a pair of Cuban-heeled boots from an ex-Samba dance champ on eBay. They've added three whole inches to my height, so it's a big "YES" from me! I'm going to be honest: they actually look utterly shite so I've also had to commission my personal tailor to produce hundreds of pairs of special boot-cut jeans to cover them up. Fabulous!'

£23.00, Ebay

A love of gloves!

Wave away those frostbite fears with this handy hint from American reader OJ.

'Whether you're defrosting your windscreen, doing a spot of gardening or simply butchering your wife, I've found there's nothing more important than a nice snug-fitting leather glove.

'Steer clear of cheap, imitation baggy woolen numbers that might slip off at any moment and get yourself some black leather finger clingers. Mine are so tight that I sometimes need to lube up my digits before entry, but it's always well worth the pain!'

£29.99, Marks and Spencer

A hard-line hairstyle!

Hairdresser supremo and national treasure Nicky Clarke tells us how to achieve this stunning look.

'It's been a tough couple of years for people's hair, but this stylish, authoritative flat-top will give you the confidence you need heading into party season. No one is going to mess with locks looking like this. And if they do, then chop off their hands LOL!

'The good news is that this funky style is so simple to create. The key here is ultimate flatness so, when you're hacking away, you'll need a high-quality spirit level from your local DIY shop. It's also important that nothing is out of place, so make sure to apply a nice thick scoop of Communist pomade, then blow-dry into a rigid, cube-like shape. Now, sit back and enjoy your newfound authority.'

£245, Nicky Clarke

KNOCK 'EM DEAD!

This season's must-have: Paedo-style specs!

This stylish retro-inspired 1970s look is all the rage at the minute. Dominic writes in to tell us about how such a simple accessory has changed his life.

'I found myself languishing in a job that I hated with little prospects for promotion. Then I bought these amazing tinted specs from Specshoppers and, before I knew it, I was heading up a large central London firm.'

£44.99, Specshoppers

Thrown Away Like ROTTING

*My Piers thought he'd met the girl of his dreams.
What she did next I can never forgive!*
By Gabrielle, 76, from Surrey

Me with Piers. Happier times

Ask any mother what her biggest fear is and she'll tell you it's the thought of her children suffering. I'm no different, so you can imagine my horror when a vicious woman trampled on my son.

It seemed like Meghan had walked into Piers' life at just the right moment. He'd been having a tough time at work and things were beginning to really get on top of him. There'd been some kind of a mix up with the office answer machine messages and poor Piers had taken the blame. The story had even made the local gazette. 'You know what the papers are like mum, full of lies!' Piers had told me on more than one occasion. I kept telling myself, 'Don't worry Gab, your brave little soldier will pull through.' But deep down I knew this wasn't true.

Then things took a turn for the worse. He'd been best friends with an American boy called Donald for years. Donald was a difficult child, and most of the other mums wouldn't let their kids play with him. I even remember one mother describing Donald

as a 'spoiled little cunt' one afternoon. But Piers seemed to love him, and that was all that mattered. So, when Piers came home and told me they weren't speaking anymore, I was devastated. Without any friends or work to keep him busy, he started falling apart in front of me. At first, it seemed quite nice to have him around the house. But the novelty soon wore off. He became addicted to various daytime TV shows. *Homes Under the Hammer* was his favourite and he would sit there in just his dressing gown, eating Pop-Tarts and watching it on loop day after day. 'I met Dion Dublin once,

> **Without any friends or work... he started falling apart**

you know, Mum?' He would shout every time the ex-Coventry City target man came on screen. As you can imagine, I was beside myself with worry.

Then one day he told me he'd made a new friend online. He said her name was Meghan, she was from America and that he was totally besotted with her. I hadn't seen him so happy for months. Finally, things seemed to be looking up.

He said he had arranged to meet her for a drink and that he wanted to look his best. It was like magic and overnight he began to transform himself. He would do press-ups, squats and burpees morning, noon and night. I'd catch him standing in front of the mirror,

practising jokes and funny anecdotes, or shadow boxing to the *Airwolf* theme tune. He even got dressed some days.

On the day he met her, he was more nervous than I've ever seen him. As a treat, I whipped up his favourite lunch: Finders Crispy Pancakes and Alphabetti Spaghetti. But when I called him, he said: 'I don't think I'll be able to hold anything down, Mum.' Then he ran back upstairs and did more exercising. He was groaning and moaning all afternoon before it was finally time to pack him off for his big night out.

When he got home from the date later that night, he was ecstatic. 'Mummy, I've met the one, Mummy, I've met the one,' he kept shouting. 'Oh, Piers,' I said, grabbing him into a tight hug. 'I'm so proud!' Finally, my boy was back on track, and with a beautiful American of all people.

Piers' happiest moment

a Piece of MEAT

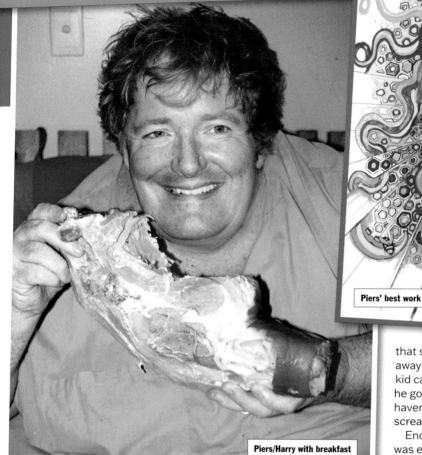

Piers/Harry with breakfast

Piers' best work

Unhealthy obsession

But the very next morning, things began to go wrong. Piers had messaged Meghan 38 times during the night, and she hadn't responded once. By 10am he was in floods of tears. It didn't look good. He kept checking his phone and asking me to see if there were any answer messages on the landline, but I knew the signs only too well. That American floozy had taken my boy for a ride.

The following days were absolutely heart-breaking. I could hear him through the walls screaming out at night and manically punching his pillows. He would shout out the same name over and over as he pummelled away. 'HARRY! HARRY! HARRY!'

I suggested he phone a helpline for advice and I crouched on the landing so I could listen. 'Hello, is that Childline?' he asked, before telling them everything. He was mostly crying, but in between gulps he explained how he had met the girl of his dreams but that she had run off straight away with some rich ginger kid called Harry. 'What's he got that I haven't?!' he screamed.

Enough was enough I thought. I'd seen an advert in the local paper for a spiritual healer named Mr Latif. He promised to fix any relationship problems by encouraging his clients to tackle their demons through artistic expression. Well, that sounded good to me. When Piers returned from his session with Mr Latif, he was different somehow. There was no more screaming or crying. He seemed cold and disengaged. 'I am about to embark on a spiritual journey, Mother,' he explained. This involved

locking himself in his room for a month, eating only red meat and drinking full-fat milk. I was totally forbidden from entering his bedroom and could only communicate with him via notes slid under the door.

By the end of the month, I was in pieces. I hadn't seen my little boy's face in weeks and even though I knew he was alive – I could hear him rummaging around in his room – it felt like he was dead. Then, one day, I just snapped! I stormed up the stairs, and without saying a word, kicked his bedroom door wide open. It almost flew off the hinges. What I saw that afternoon upon entering his room will never ever leave me. From floor to ceiling, the walls were covered in paintings of Meghan. He must have drawn hundreds of them. But worse than that, he was absolutely enormous. He must've weighed 25 stone. And, to top it off, he'd dyed his hair ginger. 'Piers, my darling, what have you done to yourself?' I screamed. 'I identify as Harry now, Mother,' he replied, as he took another bite out of a giant hunk of meat.

There's no happy ending to my story. They talk about the American dream but, for me and Piers/Harry, it was a pure American nightmare.

> **From floor to ceiling, the walls were covered in paintings of Meghan**

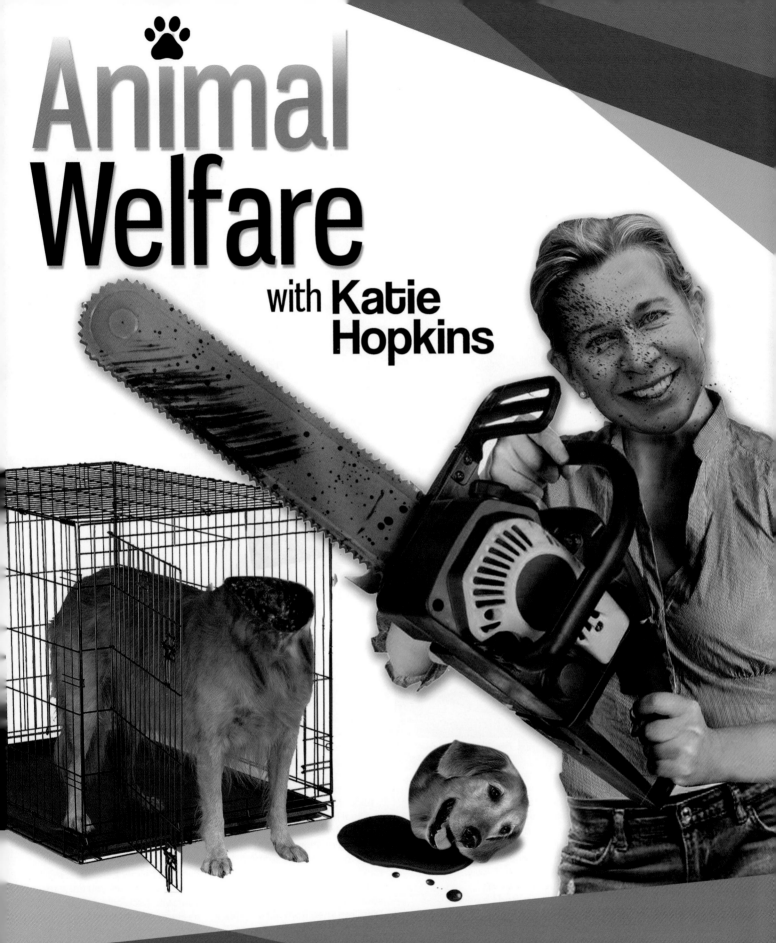

Win!

Your chance to win a KILLER ROBOT!

Explosive Puzzle!

E asily settle disputes with pesky neighbours by winning this top of the range killing machine worth over £18.5m!

We've teamed up with a dynamic Boston-based robotics company to offer our readers this incredible murdering mutt. The Manhunter ZX500 is a state-of-the-art military-grade termination unit with easy set-up for all your stalking and elimination needs. This deadly machine's animal-like behaviour will electrify its lucky new owner, and, like all death robots in this fast-growing and exciting new field, it's explosive!

With a top running speed of 15 metres per second, this puppy could outsprint Usain Bolt on steroids. Not only that, its impressive biting power of 7000 pounds per square inch means any opponent will be mutilated! Deirdre at number 26 is truly fucked.

But the Manhunter ZX500 is more than just a morbid killing toy. Its sophisticated, cutting-edge artificial intelligence is programmed to replicate the behaviour of man's best friend. That's right! Say goodbye to scooping shit off the lawn or expensive trips to the vet, and say hello to your new family pet. Your kids will love playing with the Manhunter and your wife will thank you for keeping your home safe from ANY intruder! And just imagine him tearing the head off a 'staffy' down your local park! Fun! Fun! Fun!

3 letter word
Bug

4 letter words
Beta, Code, Copy, Data, Gear

5 letter words
Agent, Droid, Smart

6 letter words
Design, Gadget, Orders, System, Upload

7 letter words
Robocop, Servant

8 letter word
Dystopia

9 letter words
Automaton, Destroyer

10 letter word
Industrial

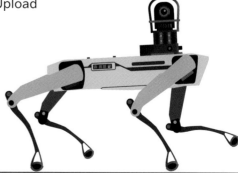

Out Of This World!

I got more than I bargained for when my new man promised to show me the stars.

By Debbie Horton, 48, from St Helens

His true form REVEALED!

As the spaceship left Earth's atmosphere, Mark dug his fingernails into his skin and began to rip it off. Whenever a relationship goes weird, you look back and suddenly notice warning signals along the way. With Mark, there were plenty.

It all started when I took my PC to be fixed. It was riddled with viruses because my ex, Tony, had been downloading weird stuff like bomb-making manuals and farm porn. He was a white supremacist and, to be fair, I was glad to see the back of him.

I took my computer to a local shop, A&E for your PC, and a really cool American called Mark said he could fix it in no time.

He was gorgeous: straight away I noticed his smooth, rubbery skin and goggle-eyes, which reminded me of my cousin Sandra's pet lizard. A happy memory.

As he worked on my computer, he told me about his life. 'I'm an American exchange student.

Me with sexy Mark

I've got big plans and I'd love to take you out and tell you about them.'

I wasn't really looking for anything serious but I'm always up for a bit of fun, and I can't lie, I was flattered that this young man would show such an interest in an older woman.

We started dating and it didn't take long for it to become obvious that Mark was a bit… different. I

Mark was a bit… different

love my food: curries, kebabs, Chinese, all that. But I noticed Mark never ate or drank anything.

I confronted him about it one night and he said: 'I only eat animals that I've caught and killed myself.'

I then started noticing my kitchen bin was always full of perfectly clean piles of bones. Looking back, this coincided with a lot of

In retrospect, I should have seen it coming

Me now

pets going missing around my neighbourhood. But I was determined to not be a bigot like Tony, so I tried to not be judgemental of Mark's culture.

Mark would call other people 'humanoids' or 'primitive sentient Earth dwellers', which did seem a bit odd. But I thought maybe that's just how Americans talk. He told me that he planned to enslave the planet with this dead clever computer program he was making called the Book of Face. Lads will be lads, I thought.

One day he turned to me and said, 'Debbie, I want you to be my Lizard Queen, sat next to me on my throne as I rule the planet.' I wasn't ready to settle down so I thought about ending it there and then, but the truth is, sex with Mark was out of this

'Debbie, I want you to be my Lizard Queen'

world.

He had this proper long, scaly tongue, and let's just say he really knew how to use it. Not like Tony – his stubby little tongue wouldn't go anywhere near there. He reckoned that only woke Marxists went 'south of the border'.

So I decided to keep my thing with Mark going a little bit longer. In no time at all,

he said he wanted me to meet his parents. I said: 'I think it's a bit soon for that love,' but he wasn't having it. Suddenly, a giant spacecraft appeared in the sky above my flat. It really was something, and before I knew what was going on, it sucked us both up through a ray of intense light.

Aboard the spaceship, I wanted to tell Mark that maybe we needed to have a bit of time apart, but I got distracted when he started ripping off his skin. That's when the penny dropped:

Mark was an alien!

He had this weird reptilian shape and his parents came in and they were reptiles too. They slid into the room and kept flicking their tongues out of their mouths. It was all so weird.

Naturally, I was dead worried at this stage – mainly because I realised my Mum and Dad weren't going to approve at all. They hated foreigners so goodness knows what they would think of aliens.

As I write this, I'm still trapped on the spaceship. The food isn't great, and I've had to survive on a diet of live mice mainly. What I'd give for a keema naan and a chicken jalfrezi. But I can't complain too much. The wi-fi up here is amazing, and Mark has got his Book of Face thing up and running and he reckons it's only a matter of time before I can start talking with people I hated at school. Happy days!

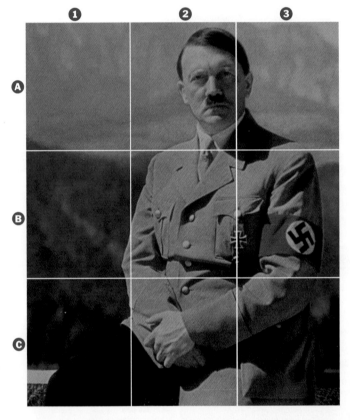

Reader's Tips 'n' Tricks!

Bright ideas from YOU!

I was sick and tired of Illuminati commie paedo lizards melting my brain with 5G radiation all the time, so I made this clever protective hat by re-using the discarded tin foil from my Sunday roast. It looks great and is a really nice snug fit on my big, fat melon head.
Alex Jones, 47, Texas, USA

COMMIES FOILED

After watching *Love Island* I really wanted some big juicy botox lips but wasn't willing to fork out all that money on a real plastic surgeon. I just covered my lips with jam and lay down next to a wasps' nest at the end of my garden. It was a bit painful, but well worth it!
Gemma Fisher, 28, Suffolk

Life-Coach Certified!

I was having real trouble disguising what a passive-aggressive highly-strung self-centred bitch I am to all my friends, so I re-trained as a yoga teacher. Now they think I'm really calm and spiritual. I've also set up an Instagram account as a 'Life Coach', which helps create the illusion that I've got my life together in some way.
Michelle Watson, 36, Hemel Hempstead

SUCKY! SUCKY!

During last summer's heatwave, my local Asda ran out of ice lollies, so I simply made my own by filling condoms with Robinson's orange squash. The kids were over the moon and my husband was glad to see them finally put to good use, too.
Irene Bryant, 39, Birmingham

WELL BALANCED!

TIP of the Week

If you're in need of a few extra quid then catch some cats in your local area and wait for the owners to offer a reward if you find them. It's a really easy way to make ends meet, and great fun if you're a cat lover like me! The best way to lure them in is to crush some Nytol into a big bowl of Whiskas cat food left just outside your back door.
Maureen Mulcock, 76, Hereford

GETTING LIPPY

CAT NAPPING

MISSING!
TABBY CAT WITH GREEN EYES
HIS NAME IS: TIDDLES

£50 REWARD!
PLEASE CALL SYLVIA 0203 026 2491

'Get off the FENCE!'

I wouldn't let my rare condition hold me back! It was a fight but, eventually, I found happiness.
By Keir, 58, from Oxted, Surrey

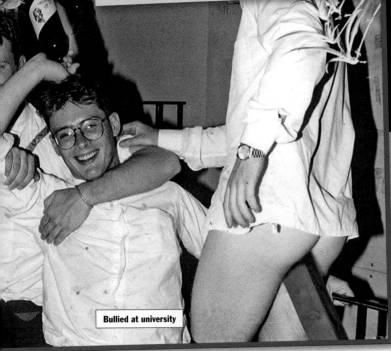

Bullied at university

O ver the years, I've heard all the jokes and barbs. People tell me to 'get off the fence', they ask me if my favourite sport is fencing, and then they start singing 'Don't Fence Me In'.

Let me take you back to the start. I was born with a rare disorder that meant, by the age of four, I had a perfectly formed square wooden fence post growing out of my anus. You can imagine how difficult this made my childhood. I was bullied every day.

I wasn't allowed to play football like all the other boys. Instead, I was used as one of the goalposts. I felt awful when I saw all the other lads enjoying themselves, while I had to sit up there, terrified one of the bullies would kick the ball at me. I wouldn't have been able to get out of the way.

I returned home crying so many times. My parents were continually taking me to the hospital for operations.

> **I was used as one of the goalposts**

Sometimes the doctors would be able to remove the fence post and I'd think my ordeal was over. The trouble was, they couldn't remove the root, so it would just grow back.

I do have one happy memory, however. It was a windy February in 1975 and the fence blew over in the school playground.

There was a dangerous paedophile on the loose in the area at the time and the teachers said it was too risky for the kids to be out in the playground with no fence. That's when Reg Meadows, the school caretaker, took me to one side and suggested that we use my anal post to hold up the broken fence. It worked, and I still remember how amazing it felt being sat at the top of the post watching all the other kids playing safely down below, thanks to me. I loved the feeling of helping people.

That was the best day of my life and the bullies left me alone afterwards. I became semi-popular for a while and even got my first kiss from a girl with a glass eye called Marie Edwards. I can still remember her mouth tasting like tinned meat.

But there was no disguising the fact that I still had a huge wooden fence post sticking out of my backside. As I grew older, unfortunately, the bullying started up again.

I managed to get a place at the prestigious Oxford University, and instantly joined the debating society. I was popular on my first day. People said I was replacing a guy who was too angry and left-wing, and that it was great to have 'a grown-up' back in the room. I decided very early on that I would always stay calm and forensic in the debates. Rather than choosing a clearly defined side, I would try to see both sides of the argument. I couldn't understand why this wouldn't be popular, but people kept

Me aged nine

Dr Gupta says:

shouting: 'Get off the fence, Keir!'

There was a group of really posh boys who were particularly vicious to me. They'd all laugh and jeer whenever I spoke. They threw rotten eggs at me, drew rude pictures on my back and regularly beat me up. But for some reason, they were always more popular than me, which I could never understand.

When I left uni, I worked as a barrister for a while but, whenever I used the word 'offence' in court, everyone laughed at me. I don't know why.

Anyway, now I'm proud to have a big, important job in central London. I chose a job that takes me back to that happy day at school; basically, every day now, I sit on the fence and look down at everyone.

> **Every day now, I sit on the fence and look down at everyone**

I'm happily married and I have two children. I've even got a few quid in the bank so, every morning, a carpenter called Marius comes round to sand down my fencepost before I leave for work. If only the haters could see me now.

Me now. Happy and content!

BREXIT BETTY DOES BRITAIN!

Our **Betty** is travelling the length and breadth of the **UK** spreading the Brexit gospel. If you manage to spot her in your town, village or city, send us a pic and you could be in with a chance of winning a wonderful **Festival of Brexit** tea towel **worth** **£15.00!***

*Please do not approach or interact directly with Betty. She can be violent and dangerous.

BREXIT BETTY DOES BRITAIN
Have a Wank

Win!
Festival of Brexit
Tea Towel

Knickers in a Twist

I was walking past the launderette at the end of my road and noticed Betty washing her dirty knickers. It was such a thrill to have a real celeb in the area.

Maureen Townsend, 37, from Walsall

Express Delivery

I spotted Betty reading the paper on a park bench while I was walking my dog, Boris. She was reading the *Express* which is my favourite newspaper, too. Yay!

Sylvia Moss, 43, from Hartlepool

Ice Maiden

I got this pic of Betty buying a lovely joint of frozen gammon from the Iceland in town. I wanted to say hello, but I've got quite a dark complexion so I thought better of it.

Carol Morris, 56, from Barnsley

Buttylicious

I was so honoured to see Betty eating her breakfast in my local caff, Harry's. We've had quite a few Muslims move to the area recently, so I was also pleased to see she was enjoying a bacon sandwich.

Mike Hunt, 64, from Barnsley

Out Dogging

Like all British patriots, I'm a real dog lover. I was snapping some really cuddly pups when Betty walked past. I couldn't believe my luck!

Phyliss Watkins, 74, from Great Yarmouth

High Roller

I've been in and out of rehab for my gambling addiction for years now, so you can imagine the boost I got when I saw Betty sat at the FOBT in my local Betfred's.

Robert Hennessy, 47, from Dudley

Pump Action

I eyed Betty filling up her car at my local petrol station. She was smoking a cigarette, which was a bit naughty, so I suggested that she extinguish it. That didn't go down too well, but she voted for Brexit, so she's still a legend in my book!

Karen Hughes, 29, from Doncaster

Mummy, there's an elf living at the end of our GARDEN!

Me and my girls

I thought my new house was a paradise, and my little girls loved it. I could have never predicted the pain and anguish that awaited.
Julie Padstow, 37, from Harrogate.

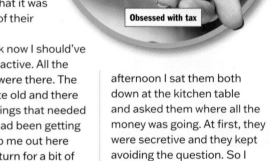

Obsessed with tax

When the letter confirming my divorce hit the doormat, I could feel every part of my body relax. I was finally turning the page and putting those seven horrible years behind me. My ex-husband, Sean, liked a drink but a drink didn't like Sean: the moment he had a drink in him, the fists came out. Night and day I was terrified of what he might do to me or our two little girls, Molly and Polly.

So you can imagine the relief when I finally got Sean out of my life. I started to enjoy myself again and soon moved to a lovely new house on a leafy street in Harrogate. I even got a new haircut: my freedom fringe, I called it. Life seemed perfect.

As for Molly and Polly, they were so happy. The house had an enormous garden with a little stream at the back and they would be out there playing almost every day. The sound of their laughter echoing through the trees is the sort of soundtrack every mum wants to hear, isn't it?

One day, I caught Molly looking worried and I asked her what was the matter. She said that she and Polly had met an elf-like creature by the stream. His name was The Rishi and they played with him every day. At first, I assumed they were making it up. You know what kids are like.

Over the next few weeks, they both became completely obsessed with The Rishi. Molly would spend every moment she wasn't in the garden doing creepy drawings of him and making up little songs. Polly, the elder of the two, said she had a crush on him and began referring to him as Dishy Rishi. It was starting to become a

> **'If I just paid The Rishi his tax, things would be ok'**

bit much, but I kept telling myself that it was just a figment of their imaginations.

Looking back now I should've been more proactive. All the warning signs were there. The house was quite old and there were a lot of things that needed fixing up, so I had been getting the girls to help me out here and there in return for a bit of pocket money.

'There you go,' I'd say, handing them a crisp £5 note. 'Go to the corner shop and buy yourself some treats.'

But, after a while, I realised they never seemed to buy anything with the money. I never once saw them with even a bar of chocolate. While they were at school, I checked in their room and there was no sign of any new toys or clothes.

When they got home that afternoon I sat them both down at the kitchen table and asked them where all the money was going. At first, they were secretive and they kept avoiding the question. So I shone a torch in their faces and shouted: 'Answer the question!'

That's when Polly opened up. She said The Rishi was making them give him the money as tax. She even showed me a letter he had given them, with 'FINAL DEMAND' printed on it in red. I ran to the toilet and threw up. How could I have been so stupid?

'That's it!' I bellowed, 'No more playing in the garden and no more fucking Rishi!' They both burst into tears and I felt like a terrible mum for swearing, but enough was enough. The

Me now. Strong and independent

Molly and the Rishi

Molly's drawing of the Rishi

'Looking for me, Julie?'

I turned, and there he was, the famous Rishi. I should've been scared but I was totally calm. Why? Because he was absolutely tiny. He looked so big in the drawings but, in reality, he was a tiny midget elf. I grabbed a plant pot and kicked him under it, then transferred him to an old hessian sack that was lying about in the shed. I drove up to a local canal, filled the sack with bricks and threw him in. Easy! I'd seen off Sean, now I'd dealt with the Rishi.

On the way home, I stopped for a glass of wine in a country pub. It was time to celebrate my freedom again. As I was leaving, I was approached by an old Chinese man who was selling a sort of strange puppy-like

back door was kept locked at all times and I signed up to a Disney Plus subscription to keep them entertained. I hoped that would be the end of it but things just got weirder.

One night, the electricity, gas and water got cut off. Next, the internet went down. Winter was setting in and before long we were all huddled under a blanket shivering. I didn't know what to do. Molly and Polly kept

telling me that, if I just paid The Rishi his tax, things would be ok. If not, he would get angry and take our house away. Not for the first time in my life, I was cornered. It was time to confront this monster.

I grabbed a large knife from the kitchen drawer, did a shot of vodka to steady my nerves, kissed my girls, then unlocked the back door. As I crept slowly down the garden, the wind

began to howl like a rabid wolf. Eventually, I reached the banks of the icy stream. I scanned the area intently, clutching the knife tightly in my sweaty palms. 'What was I doing?' I thought. It all seemed so ridiculous. Then I heard a voice behind me.

creature for £30. 'What a bargain!' I thought, and bought it for the girls to cheer them up. As I drove away he mumbled something about water and midnight but by then I had my stereo on full blast. It was time to turn the page again.

Pest Control!
with Darren

Someone has to come out and say it: pests are annoying around the house. We all want to keep our families safe, so here's your guide to controlling the most dangerous pests around.

Bees

Make sure you kill all the bees in your garden. They make an annoying buzzing sound and they might sting you at any moment. You just can't trust them.

By the way, don't be fooled by the 'woke' mainstream media who try to trick you into believing that we need bees for the planet to survive. This is just a leftie conspiracy so the middle-class elite can sit eating honey together and being all smug.

Birds

I saw a post on Facebook that said foreign birds are outbreeding the UK's native birds by 15 to 1. Apparently, these invading, coloured varieties are stealing nests from white, British birds.

It's time for a cull. Soak breadcrumbs in a strong British alcohol, such as gin, then scatter the crumbs over your lawn and sit back and watch as the birds gobble them up and get drunk. You can then easily finish them off with a cricket bat or a golf club. Sorted.

Butterflies

Did you know that some butterflies are born with both male and female sex organs? How pathetic is that? It's like, make your mind up!

The last thing any hard-working family needs is a butterfly corrupting their young into the trans agenda. So unless you want your David to become Deirdre, kill butterflies on sight. A rolled-up tabloid paper will do the trick.

Fish

Kill all fish by pouring tonnes of bleach into any rivers or lakes near your house. There's literally nothing worse than having fish nibbling around your ankles when you're paddling.

Also, we don't know the country of origin of half of these fish that illegally wash up on our shores. They could easily be aquatic Jihadi terrorists, intent on turning our blue, British waters into an Islamic caliphate.

Trees

Pest Invaders!

Do you want some smelly Extinction Rebellion type in your garden? I mean, obviously not! Then you must poison any trees in your yard, or you'll soon have some dreadlocked do-gooder called Tristan handcuffing himself to one of them.

Trees also block sunlight and are breeding grounds for many pests. So kill them all today.

The WEDDING

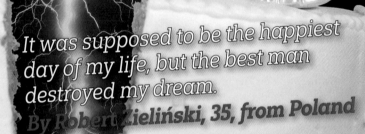

It was supposed to be the happiest day of my life, but the best man destroyed my dream.
By Robert Zieliński, 35, from Poland

Me with Jeremy

As a boy growing up in Warsaw, I would try to imagine my wedding day. I would picture smiling faces, confetti in the air, and everyone cheering my wife and I as we set off for our new life together. I didn't expect to be taken away in handcuffs. But that's exactly what happened after I made the biggest mistake of my life.

From the moment I arrived in England, I worked longer hours than you can imagine. I was a security guard at an expensive new apartment block next to the River Thames in London. Every day, I'd be up before dawn and I never got home before midnight. Every night I would collapse into bed.

One day on my way home from work, I met a girl called Sarah. She was the most beautiful girl I had ever seen, and I could hardly believe my luck when she gave me her number. It was love at first sight, as you say in England.

We began seeing each other, and I was determined not to lose her, so one day I went down on one knee and asked her if she'd be my wife. I nearly fainted when she said yes. I was the happiest man in the world.

I wanted the day to be special so I spent a year planning the event. Sarah said that her family had no money so I would have to pay for it all myself. I asked my boss if I could do overtime, then started saving almost every penny I earned to pay for the wedding. I went without

> **I nearly fainted when she said yes**

lunch for a whole year! As my stomach rumbled away every afternoon, I told myself it would be worth it, and would also help me lose a bit of weight, so I would be more desirable for my beloved Sarah.

As the wedding day approached, I realised that I didn't have a best man. I would have loved to ask my brother, Ryszard, but he had been murdered earlier that year. And I didn't really have any friends here in the UK.

Then suddenly out of nowhere, I struck up a friendship with a guy called Jeremy who lived in the building where I worked. Whenever he passed through reception, he would stop for a quick chat. Before long he started to feel like a second brother to me.

I decided I would ask him if he would be my best man.

'I wouldn't have thought so mate,' he said when I asked him, and started laughing. I felt sad and embarrassed. But then I showed him a picture of Sarah and he suddenly changed his mind. 'Hmmm she looks alright doesn't she, eh?

Love at first sight

SMASHER!

Jeremy at my wedding

'faithful' and all hell broke loose. Jeremy shouted: 'But can you even spell "faithful", Robert?' Everyone laughed. Then he started asking where I'd got the flowers from and whether everything was 'above board'.

He ran out to his car and came back holding a lie detector machine. He grabbed me and strapped me into it. Then he asked: 'You're a love rat, aren't you, Robert? Tell the truth: did you once snog Sarah's sister, Jane? The truth, Robert!'

I said it was only a five-second kiss and that it had been a chance encounter six months before I even met Sarah, but the light on the machine started flashing. Then Jeremy and the guests all pointed at me and shouted: 'Liar! Liar! Liar!'

There was worse to come. He stood right in front of me with his face pressed against mine. I could smell his oniony breath as he asked: 'Robert, did you fill in a "Right to Remain" form after Brexit?'

I gulped and said yes. The guests were already hissing. Even my gran was joining in. Then Jeremy whipped out a form from his pocket and showed the crowd that I'd ticked the wrong box when I filled it in.

'Do you know what that means?' he asked. 'You're an illegal immigrant, matey!'

Then he clicked his fingers and two border police guards grabbed me and started dragging me back down the aisle. Everyone was chanting: 'Out! Out! Out!' The last thing I saw as the church doors closed was Jeremy putting his arm around Sarah to console her. She seemed to be enjoying it.

> '**You're a love rat, aren't you, Robert?**'

Okay, I'll do it,' he said. 'I'd love to meet Sarah, she looks like a right laugh.'

Finally, the big day arrived. It was lucky that I had saved up so much money because Sarah's family wasn't just poor – it was also huge. She had over 100 people on the guest list. To be fair they all looked amazing. Even her baby nephews were dressed in little grey suits with pink bow ties. I've never seen such a smartly dressed family.

I only had two guests. The first was my grandmother. She is 103 and on an oxygen tank. She'd flown over from Warsaw especially for the big day.

My other guest was Jeremy but, just as we were due to begin, I received a text message from him telling me he'd be late. We all sat and waited. Then finally, after nearly two hours, he arrived.

As soon as he walked in he began to act really strangely. He kept getting up and strutting around the church like he was the star of the show. He would sit in random seats and shout abuse at me, even while I was saying my vows.

When I said I would 'love and cherish' Sarah, he shouted: 'Are you sure about that?' The strange thing was that he very quickly got everyone in the church on his side. I could feel the room turning against me.

Then I promised to be

Me now

Amazing Beauty
advice from our readers

Go from bald to BOLD!

Andrew, 72, from Paisley, Scotland tells us about how obscuring his baldness gave him the confidence to be a complete cunt.

'When my hair started falling out I lost all my confidence. Overnight, I went from a stallion of a man who was wolf-whistled by women wherever I went to someone barely noticed as I waddled down the street.

'Well, all that changed when I started using a remarkable contraption. It's called a wig and it covers up your baldness convincingly. No one will know the difference.

'And the best part is that my wig doubles up as a Brillo pad, so the wife is always happy when it's my turn to do the dishes. Fab!'

BEFORE

AFTER

• Cherry Blossom Boot Polish: available at www.amazon.co.uk £2.99
• McDonald's Banana Milkshake: (Regular) £1.69 via McDonald's app
• Heavy Duty Scouring Pads (24 pack): available at www.amazon.co.uk £12.99

BANISH those bags!

George, 49, from London, has a special tip for how to remove bags from under your eyes.

'If you've had too many late nights and those dark circles under your eyes just won't go away, then I've found the perfect solution. Simply place the hearts of two poverty-ridden children over your eyes for half an hour before bed. Just remember to wash off the blood before you go to sleep.

'So whether you're a party animal or you're simply missing out on some winks because the guilt of stealing money from poor and sick people is keeping you awake at night (definitely the former for me, but everyone's different), then this is the wonder treatment you need. It's to die for!'

Get a perfect tan on a budget

Justin, 49, from Canada, can help you get that exotic tan look without breaking the bank.

'With our hectic lifestyles these days it's hard to get an authentic, rich tan without spending half the year on holiday. Chance would be a fine thing, right?

'But I found a simple, cheap solution: simply smear boot polish all over your face and body. Once you get used to the smell it's brilliant! It certainly gets you lots of attention!'

TRY THIS

Wave bye-bye to nasty skin

Tommy, 38 from Luton, writes in:

'I struggled for years with oily, spotty Nazi – sorry, I mean nasty – skin. I started getting really angry with the world and leaving trolling comments under *Daily Mail* articles.

'One day, someone threw a McDonald's vanilla milkshake at me. I thought my life was over but then the next day I woke up with a perfect complexion!'

• Unless otherwise stated, all products are available on the high street.

Get Your Family PUMPED UP

Kiss goodbye to your embarrassing scrawny kids and kick your pathetic flabby partner to the kerb! It's time to say hello to your new life with a pumped-up brood of stunning muscle beasts! That's right, Have a Wank is offering one lucky reader the ultimate self-improvement package with this lifetime supply of anabolic steroids for the WHOLE family!

Simply fill out the word puzzle opposite with the aid of the body's least impressive muscle – the brain – and you can win the chance to get jacked every day of your life without ever needing to break a sweat again!

What's included in the giveaway:
Oral: Anadrol, Anavar, Dianabol, Winstrol and Restandol.
Injectable: Deca-Durabolin, Durabolin, Depo-Testosterone, Agovirin, Retandrol and Equipoise.

The author and publishers don't actually endorse taking steroids!

Stick it in to win!

P O W E R

FINISHED? Call the competition hotline now!
0203 026 2491*

*Not a real competition

3 letter words
Bro, Gym, Max

4 letter words
Core, Curl, Edge, Form, Sets, Tone

5 letter words
Chalk, Clamp, Elbow, EZ bar, Power, Press, Sinew

6 letter words
Banned, Growth, Muscle

7 letter words
Bulking, Incline, Spotter, Steroid, Stretch, Testing, Vitamin, Workout

8 letter words
Deltoids, Dumbbell, Olympian, Progress

9 letter words
Abdominal, Isolation, Medicinal

10 letter word
Supplement

11 letter word
Therapeutic

12 letter word
Testosterone

Driven to MADNESS!

All I wanted was to buy a new car, but a sick and twisted bully was waiting to pounce!
By Tim Whelan, 18, from Oxfordshire

Jeremy my tormentor

Pork scratchings and a pint

I introduced myself. He immediately bought me a pint of ale. Maybe he was trying to be friendly, but when I told him I don't drink, he got really angry.

'You're not one of those vegan twats, are you?' he growled. 'Oooh, I only eat celery and drink chia seed smoothies because I'm a vegan twat that plays with his little willy and drives a Vauxhall Corsa.'

I'm actually not vegan, which was lucky because he stuck a handful of pork scratchings into my mouth. Then he ordered me to drink some of 'the finest ale that Oxfordshire has to offer'.

I was actually quite scared, and often find it's easier not to disobey people like him. So I started to guzzle down the brown, foamy pint. It stank of urine and tasted like I would imagine bog water tastes.

I started losing track of time. The next thing I knew it was late afternoon and Jeremy had taken his shirt off. He had these grotesque, saggy man boobs.

But he seemed happy that I was drinking ale. 'There you

go, you already look like a man that drives an Alfa Romeo GTV6,' he said. Then he slapped me on the back, stood up and shouted: 'Now come with me!'

Everyone in the pub looked relieved when we left but, for me, my nightmare was just beginning.

It was already getting dark when we stumbled out onto the muddy country lane and started making our way towards Jeremy's farm.

It wasn't a long walk but he suddenly stopped in his tracks and shouted: 'This is where I like to crap!' He squatted down under a tree and pulled his jeans down around his big wellies. He didn't seem to care who saw him.

'Look at me, Tim, I'm doing a dump! I bet you can't dump as good as me can you?' he said gleefully. It was like watching

I was in my first year at university and, like for most students, money was really tight. All I wanted was a nice little car to get me from A to B, so when I saw the advert in the local paper my eyes lit up. It read: 'Almost new Ford Focus just £300.' What a deal, I thought. It seemed too good to be true – and believe me, it was!

The ad was from a guy called Jeremy. I phoned the number and this growling voice answered. I felt a bit intimidated but I said I was calling about the car and he said I should come to his farm to pick it up. I couldn't get there quickly enough.

When I arrived, I was surprised to see the place was called Diddly Squat Farm. That

should have been a heads-up but I was so desperate for the car I ignored it. It feels stupid, looking back.

There was a note from Jeremy pinned to the fence, telling me to meet him in the local pub – The Tite Inn. When I walked in, I saw this awful, pissed bloke. He was staggering around, emptying out every packet of pork scratchings into a big muddy bucket.

Then he started parading around the pub, with a cigarette in his mouth, handing out free pork scratchings and saying: 'I'm fucking loaded, I'm fucking loaded!' I'd met his type before and they always scare me.

> **'You're not one of those vegan twats, are you?'**

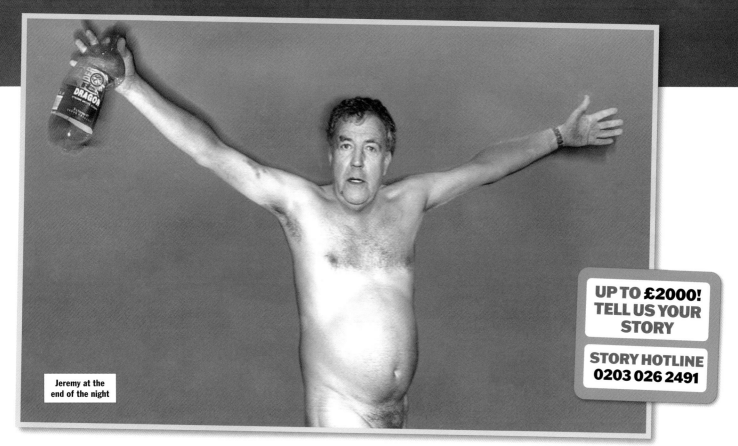

Jeremy at the
end of the night

an animal, but what he did next would shame any beast.

He started to alternate between eating a pork scratching and then ramming a pork scratching up his filthy behind. He looked almost furious as he chanted: 'One for me and one for you, one for me and one for you.'

I was so scared by now that I decided to just run for it, but I was really drunk and kept falling over. Suddenly, I heard Jeremy laughing and running after me. He was shouting: 'I'm coming for you, Timmy, my boy!'

Before I knew it, he had me face down in the mud and everything went black. When I came to, we were at Jeremy's farm, sitting in front of a bonfire. He was completely naked and I could see he had tied the car keys to the end of his penis.

He was spouting off about the car's performance and belching out little facts about how well it handles corners. He said I would love the car and that he would even be prepared to knock £150 off the price, but only on one condition.

He led me into a barn where some sheep were sleeping. He said he would half the price as long as I retrieved the keys after he had hidden them. 'Just a bit of fun,' he said, but I froze in horror on seeing his next move.

He woke up his favourite sheep, Barbara, and shoved the keys deep inside her backside. The way he did it was far from romantic. He made me hand over the cash and then he walked back to the house to drink port and eat cheese while he watched me trying to get the keys out of Barbara.

There I was, on my hands and knees, with my hand up a sheep's backside

There I was, on my hands and knees, with my hand up a sheep's backside. I could hear Jeremy laughing and cheering. Barbara kept kicking me.

Finally, I retrieved the keys and made my way over to my new car. I put the keys in the ignition and sped away as fast as I could. But I was less than a mile down the road when I heard banging coming from the rear of the car.

I pulled over and opened the boot. To my horror, I found a little round-eyed man called Richard inside. He was wearing a French maid's outfit and was masturbating over a copy of *Auto Trader*. He looked up at me, winked and said: 'There's always room for one more, mister.'

Was it worth it?

Gastro Delights!

Now that our GREAT nation is free from the draconian EU food standard safety laws, we are finally able to embrace some of the exciting new products being imported from China.

◀ Edible Gammon Flavoured Shower Gel

from Meaty Shower Senses, £3.99

This ingenious product combines the zing of a high-quality synthetic shower gel with the succulent meaty flavour of a home-cooked joint of gammon. This great duel shower accessory allows you to either lather up to cleanse your body, or squeeze the product directly into your mouth when hunger strikes. Being able to eat and wash simultaneously is a real time saver for the busy modern Brit and, should help free up precious time for sharing migrant scare stories on Facebook or our top tip for a new network: Weibo. The wonderful gammon flavour really clings to the body for the whole day and we loved the bonus of being able to lick our own arms in the afternoon as a post-lunch treat.

Full English Breakfast ▲ Muscle Shake

from Bulldog Power, £19.99

Whether you're a builder, hungover from a boozy session, or just a fat bastard, there's nothing us patriotic Brits love more than a cooked breakfast. Now you can enjoy the great taste of a full English and get ripped at the same time with this delicious muscle shake from the scientific eggheads over at Bulldog Power. Just mix 2 large scoops of the magic powder with a pint of milk and guzzle back the goodness. We were really blown away by the rich taste of the synthesized runny egg and the authentic porky punch from the broom-handle sausage flavouring. You'll be pleased to hear that the product contains no natural ingredients whatsoever and is 100% chemical.

Parfum de Scotch Egg ▶

from Jinjiang Industry Lab, £15.99

Smelling good is what sets us Brits apart from other nations around the world, and what could smell better than a battery-farmed egg encased in a ball of processed sausage meat coated in breadcrumbs? Now, thanks to Jinjiang Industry Lab, you can radiate this wonderful pungent aroma 24/7 with a simple pump or two of a spray nozzle. The product comes beautifully packaged with eye-catching faux tartan flourishes – and is also edible! We found that three or four jets of Parfum de Scotch Egg around the neck and chest area worked wonders when trying to attract British members of the opposite sex. It also appeared to repel foreigners, which was a real unexpected bonus.

Doner Kebab in a Tin ▶

from Hangzhou Foodstuff Corp, 89p

Every proud flag-waving Brit loves to head into town on a Saturday night, drink 15 pints of Stella, smash someone's face in, then get a big greasy kebab to finish the night on the way home. Now you can enjoy a real authentic doner kebab without having to line the pockets of an immigrant shop owner. This neat, tinned alternative from Hangzhou Foodstuff Corp is so easy to prepare. Just scoop the contents of the can into a microwaveable dish and blast on max power for 3 minutes. We were really impressed with the sweaty flavour of the nondescript meat, and the soggy bread and salad brought back so many great memories from nights out over the years.

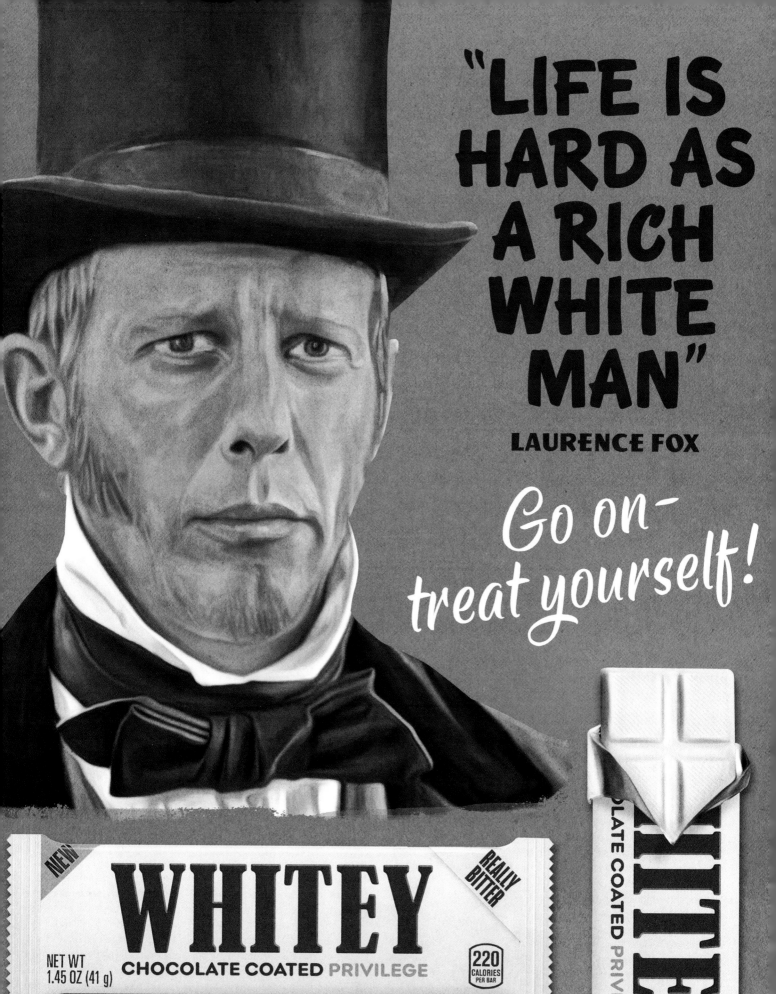

Church then back to bed!

PERIOD DRAMA!

Period PAIN!

I thought I'd met the man of my dreams, but a musty hidden secret was waiting for me in the bedroom.

By Margaret Dobson, 43, from Huddersfield

My mum always used to say she could spot a wrong 'un a mile off. I've found out the hard way that I've not been blessed with that skill.

I've always been unlucky in love. I seem to attract bastards. If there's a selfish pig out there, I'll find him. Or he'll find me.

But when I first met Jacob from Somerset I thought I'd bagged the man of my dreams. He was tall, well dressed and smelt like an antique shop. He really charmed me.

I liked his little glasses, neatly gelled side parting and especially how positive he was. Everything was 'marvellous', 'splendid' and 'super'. He made me feel so good about myself, my friends loved him and I really believed he could be 'the one'.

At first, I thought nothing of his interest in Victorian England. In fact, it seemed quite sweet and he would tell me lovely stories about what England was like before the black people arrived. But over time, I realised it was more than just a boy's hobby: it was an obsession.

The first time he came round to my place, I was surprised when he rushed straight into the bathroom. I thought, bless, he's just been caught short. But then he emerged with handfuls of my tampon packets and my knees started trembling.

'These vulgar items will have to be disposed of forthwith,' he shouted. 'I simply won't countenance you using anything but lard-coated sheep's wool for your ovulatory discharge.' He threw them in the bin and then he handed me a brown paper bag full of these weird sticky wads of wool. I didn't want to upset him, so I began using them, but they

The condoms

were absolute agony. I longed for my simple panty pads and would often catch myself singing the theme tune from the classic 1990s Bodyform advert that went:

'Ohhhhhhhh Bodyform, Bodyform for you'.

But those woollen wads turned out to be just the start of his weird demands. Before I knew it I was totally out of my depth. Sex with Jacob was bizarre. The lights had to be switched off, blackout blinds pulled down and he would only do it in the missionary position. The whole event would always last exactly 4 minutes and 30 seconds and he insisted that his penis was referred to as his 'intromittent organ'. He would count his thrusts in groups of three, with a five-second rest between each set: '1, 2, 3 and rest.'

To make matters worse he'd go into a blind rage if I made even the slightest sound, but every time he reached orgasm he would scream out: 'Oh, Nanny!' The whole thing seemed so hypocritical, but I persevered because he was such a catch.

One night I woke up and realised he wasn't next to me in bed. I assumed he must be in the toilet, but then I heard a noise coming from downstairs. It was Jacob, and he was

> **Every time he reached orgasm he would scream out: 'Oh, Nanny!'**

I thought Jacob was 'The one'

Me now

service was over he'd like us to race home and jump straight into bed.

This seemed peculiar, especially because I thought Catholics weren't allowed contraception, but he said it was okay as long as we used thick, animal-skin sheaths. They hurt and I would just stare at the ceiling, counting down the seconds until it was over.

One day, before we went to church, I threw the sheaths away when he wasn't looking. When we got home I told

I wasn't ready for kids, so I told him I wanted to go to a clinic to get the morning-after pill. He said, 'Nonsense! A girl need only trot a horse briskly over a rough road to avoid unwanted insemination'. By this point, I was petrified.

We hadn't even discussed children but now suddenly they were on the cards. He said: 'I naturally expect you to present me with at least six children.' He said he'd even decided what they would be called.

I took a deep breath and asked him to tell me the names.

'The first shall be Clemmie, the second Theodorus,' he began. 'Zebedee will be the third and the fourth shall go by Pandora. Then dost come Fennella-Loveday, and our family shall be replete when Benedictum doth arriveth.'

I didn't know what to say and my head was all over the place. Eventually, I got my breath back and said: 'Goodness…that will be a lot of nappies to change.'

'Ah yes, I've been meaning to say,' he began, 'I will never, ever, ever change a nappy. All that women's stuff is strictly the nanny's job, along with affection and intimacy.'

shouting 'Nanny!' over and over again. The alarm bells started ringing so I ran down to find out what was going on.

I opened the living room door and when I saw what was happening I nearly died. He was stood there, pyjamas around his ankles, and his face pressed against the viewfinder on an old-fashioned machine while his hand was furiously rubbing his erect intromittent organ. It was horrid and I was terrified. He hadn't noticed me so I crept back up to bed and pretended I hadn't seen anything. I Googled the machine the next day and realised it was a Victorian device for watching porn. I felt sick.

Jacob was always going on about his image at work and how important it was that I looked my best. 'It simply isn't on for me to be seen with an ugly woman,' he'd say. At night he made me strap slabs of raw meat to my face to improve my wrinkles, instead of using my Oil of Olay Night Recovery Cream. I'd also have to bathe every two weeks in a revolting cocktail of ammonia, onion juice and ambergris – the intestinal seepage of a sperm whale. I was so depressed.

Jacob was also a keen Catholic and insisted we went to church every Sunday. He said it was important to connect with Christ's message on the day of rest. As soon as the

'Just lie back and think of Albion'

him we must have run out. I was hoping this would mean we could skip the sex but he said we must do it anyway and I should 'just lie back and think of Albion.'

As he pumped away, I wondered how he ended up as a West Brom fan, but it turns out Albion is an old-fashioned word for England.

When we'd finished, I was worried that he might have got me pregnant.

Porn addict?

Have a Wank in...
SALISBURY!

This wonderful cathedral city has been welcoming travellers since 1227 – no wonder Alexander and Ruslan couldn't wait to fly over from Russia to become the latest pilgrims to this medieval metropolis.

Cathedral

The crown jewel of Salisbury is the fab cathedral, which is famous not just in Europe, but in the whole world. Alexander says: 'It's famous for its 123-metre spire, it's famous for its clock – the first one ever created in the world, which is still working.'

> 'Our friends had been suggesting for a long time that we visit this wonderful town'
> *Alexander*

A place of peace

Old fort

Further afield

No visit to Salisbury is complete without an excursion to Old Sarum. This splendid Iron Age hill fort was where the first cathedral once stood. You can stand where the Romans, Normans and Saxons all once went about their business. Brilliant for selfies!

Shopping

'Both of us love to shop until we drop,' says Ruslan with typical wit. 'So imagine how delighted we were to discover that Salisbury's global reputation as a shopping hub is well deserved.'

Alongside outlets as varied as TK Maxx and BHS, Salisbury boasts tourist favourites such as Tesco, as well as independent stores for the more pretentious visitor. There really is something for everyone.

In fact, Alexander said they were so busy flashing the plastic that they lost all track of what they had bought. 'I bought a perfume bottle for my wife but, when I started to pack, I realised I had lost it. Who knows where it ended up? I trust it didn't cause any problems!'

No spray, no lay

Nightlife

Salisbury has a growing reputation for nightlife and it's not hard to see why. With everything from cafés to restaurants, and even bars, it really is the town that never sleeps.

For those who feel even more daring, the Chapel Nightclub offers unforgettable late-night frolics. 'They played music from acts as varied as Duran Duran and Coldplay,' says Alexander. 'We jived and jived until 1am!'

What's your poison?

> ### 'Both of us love to shop until we drop'
> *Ruslan*

Rock on!

And Stonehenge is an absolute must. Here, you can walk in the footsteps of your Neolithic ancestors at the best-known prehistoric monument in Europe. 'It blew my mind to think how those big stones got there,' says Ruslan with a smile. 'I think I'm going to grow my hair out and learn the flute.'

FUN FACTS

- Salisbury has 40,302 residents!
- The population is 95.73% white!
- It stands at the confluence of three rivers: the Avon, Nadder and Bourne. How mad is that?
- It's the home of the Magna Carta!
- Would I Lie To You? brainbox David Mitchell was born here!

GYPSY CURSE!

Losing his job sent my hubby into a dark place, but I never thought he'd sink this low.
Samantha, 50, from Chipping Norton

When we were young

On hols with my man

I used to feel so proud when my husband, David, set off for work every morning. He had a high-flying job in London and drove a Jaguar car, easily the best in the village. Not only that, he was a total dish. I could just tell, as I stood there waving him off, that all our neighbours were watching and wishing they were me. I could see their curtains twitching.

He would come home after work and we'd make love while he told me stories about how much his colleagues adored him. We were living the dream! I felt like we were the envy of the world.

But I knew something was wrong when he arrived home early from work one day. His face was all red and puffy and it looked like he'd been crying. The fact he was getting out of a minicab was a giveaway. I watched him as the cab driver counted out the 8p change and I knew at that moment that my life was about to change.

'I've really messed up, sugarplum,' he said, tears streaming down his face. He explained how he'd made a giant mistake at work with an overseas deal and that he'd had to quit his job immediately. It turned out he wasn't that

popular with his colleagues after all and that the moment he screwed up they had thrown him out. Our fairytale was over, but little did I know that it was about to turn into a horror movie.

David descended into a really dark place. He was always mumbling his words and pretty much stopped looking after himself. I'd see snot all over his hands, dried up drool on his chin and he would say things like:

> **He wasn't that popular after all**

'What's the point in wiping one's bottom? Seems like a waste of time to me.' And the less said about his breath the better.

But things were about to go from bad to worse. I was stood in the kitchen one afternoon when I looked out into our garden. What I saw that day will live with me for the rest of my life. Parked at the end of our prized lawn was a caravan and David was climbing into it. 'What the hell are you doing, David?' I shouted out of the window. 'I've decided to live in this caravan and write my memoirs,' he shouted back, then slammed the door.

Caravans are my worst nightmare and for very good reason. When I was a child, a whole army of Gypsy people

arrived in caravans and parked them in one of the giant fields that my father owned behind our house. They were truly awful and Daddy told me they came from Transylvania and they were all related to Dracula. He said they never have baths, don't pay any taxes and breed like rabbits. 'It's part of their religion,' he said.

So think how I felt when I realised that my David, a man who is fifth cousin twice removed from the Queen, had decided to become a gypsy. I felt like I'd been hit by a lorry.

What made it worse was that David lived day and night in that caravan. He would barely set

foot in the house. I caught him in the kitchen one day as he was emptying a bucket down the sink. 'What are you doing?' I asked. 'Just emptying my piss and shit, darling,' he replied. It was so unlike David to swear. What had this Gypsy lifestyle done?

> **'Just emptying my piss and shit, darling'**

Things got even darker that evening. I was lying in bed having my nightly cry when I heard a blood-curdling

Me now

The filthy caravan

A 20-a-day man now

Dave and Georgey

squealing coming from the caravan. It was a truly horrific noise. I put on my dressing gown and slippers, grabbed a torch and went to investigate.

I crept down the garden and when I finally reached the caravan, I knocked on the door. 'Are you ok, David?' I shouted. No answer. My heart was racing. I slowly pushed open the door to reveal David lying in bed smiling. Next to him was a little brown pig. They were both covered in sweat and sharing a cigarette. I was so horrified and angry: David knows smoking is bad for you and yet there he was, puffing away on a cigarette

as if it was the most normal thing in the world.

'Hi Sam, meet Georgey,' he said, and then nonchalantly blew smoke rings into the air. The nerve of the man! Well, what I saw that night was nearly the end for me. I can tolerate many things, but smoking is a step too far.

What a mess. I don't know what I'll do next. I've considered leaving David, but what would people in the village think if they found out we'd divorced?

FROM RUSSIA WITH LOVE

When I went to Russia for a canoeing trip, it wasn't just 'my' boat that got wet.
By Roger, 29, from Brentford

As he peeled off his T-shirt, my eyes nearly fell out of their sockets. He had the plumpest bosoms I've ever seen. It was like they'd been inflated by a bike pump.

For a moment I thought I'd drunk too much vodka, but then I pinched one of his baps and Vladimir was definitely real.

I've always loved canoeing. I just adore that feeling when I plunge my long, narrow vessel into the wet entry point, not to mention the noise my paddles make as they smack against the surface. It's just the way I am.

> **I've been up every canal in England**

Over the years, I reckon I've been up every canal England has to offer, so when the opportunity came up to go on a canoeing adventure in Russia, I jumped at the chance.

My fellow enthusiasts and I were collected by bus at Moscow airport and our host served

Well-endowed stallion

Such a firm rod

up chilled vodka and canned sardines as we were whizzed off into the wilds of Siberia. I think it's safe to say we all felt really special.

When we arrived, our camp host, Vladimir, appeared and I nearly fell down on the spot. He was that perfect combination of someone who took pride in his appearance

but who was also a proper man.

He wore tight shirts that showed off his arm and pectoral muscles. He really was to die for.

He led us through the gates of the camp and said: 'We're going to work you really hard, and if some of you die, that won't be the first time it's happened here.' Then he laughed.

It was a really loud, deep laugh, all the way from his guts. The sort of roar that only an alpha male can produce. Try and tell me you wouldn't have fallen in love on the spot.

Every morning, Vladimir would wake us up by shaking the tents we slept in. 'Get up, or I'll send in the Cossacks,' he'd shout and then do that big laugh again. It was such fun and we never had to be told twice.

He'd lead us out on these wonderful, long days of canoeing. We whizzed around the streams and rivers of Russia, and Vladimir would be in a speedboat, bellowing orders at us.

'Come on, what are you? A man or a Muslim?' was one of his favourites. 'Go hard or go harder,' was another. I don't know how he came up with them all.

One day, we went skinny dipping in a lake. It was a freezing-cold day but it's safe to say that the temperatures didn't diminish Vladimir for a moment. Talk about a Moscow mule.

In the evenings, we would all be exhausted. Vladimir would make a barbeque and slap huge slabs of meat onto it. 'I killed this bear with my bare hands,' he would boast, and we would all giggle.

After the meal, he would always come and sit with me. He just had that way of making me feel special. It was like I was the only man in the world and I would go weak at the knees.

Well, one thing led to another and before I knew it he was showing me how to pitch his huge tent. It took me a while to get it up, but Vlad was so hands-on and knew exactly what he was doing. I was absolutely exhausted by the end of the evening and so sore I could barely walk, but it was certainly worth it to experience such an impressive erection.

Vladimir was a bit secretive. One night I noticed that his phone had 38 missed calls from a guy called 'Donny', and he insisted that we kept our relationship a secret. He assured me that he couldn't have been 'more proud' of the special thing we had going, but that if I ever told anyone then some very horrible things might happen.

And it certainly was something special! My goodness – talk about Vlad the Impaler.

Well, like Vladimir, I couldn't be more proud of my holiday romance so I want to share my story with you all. I'll never forget the guy who loved me because, for me, it was definitely from Russia with love.

Me with Vladimir

> **Before I knew it he was showing me how to pitch his huge tent**

Terrorised Lunchtime

Our dream was to open our own little artisan café, but that all changed the day Gordon walked into our lives.

By Jill, 36, from Wandsworth

It was the proudest day of our lives when Martin and I opened our little café in Wandsworth. We'd been married for nine years and had saved every penny we could to make it happen. We never had nice things like holidays or trips to restaurants or pubs like our friends did. But we had our dream, and we were determined it would come true!

And then one day we were there, opening the door to our very own little business. We called it The Wild Garden Café and, to give it an original feel, we hung works by local artists on the walls and had a rack of newspapers put up, which customers could freely browse.

I don't mind saying that Martin and I formed quite the partnership. I would be front of house, serving up delicious hot coffee and home-made banana cake to our treasured customers. Meanwhile, Martin would be behind the scenes, making heartier meals. He's a wizard in the kitchen: you should taste his home-made soups and crusty, hot sourdough bread.

But he can also turn his hand to an array of delicious lunches and dinners, including quiche, spaghetti Bolognese and – my personal favourite – Martin's famous sausage-and-onion pie. *Nom nom.*

We'd been nervous in the build-up to our opening. There was so much to arrange, and we were scared it would all go wrong. Business was slow at first, but then word got around the neighbourhood and the locals started to flock through our doors. It was a magical time.

A few months in, I started noticing a strange-looking man who was always standing across the road. He would wear a tight T-shirt, and sometimes a really crap leather jacket, as he stared intently through our window with his face all screwed up. He started turning up every day, but whenever I called Martin out to see, he would disappear. It was really unsettling.

One busy Saturday, trade was really booming, and Martin's famous sausage-and-onion pie had almost sold out. When, suddenly, the door of the café flew open and in strutted the guy in the tight T-shirt.

Seeing him up close was terrifying. He was like a weird cross between Frankenstein's monster and the Milky Bar kid on steroids. His face looked like it had been stung by a thousand wasps and then beaten with a rusty crowbar before being caked in make-up. It was horrific!

Normally, customers wait to be seated, but he swaggered straight to a table, muttering about 'crap décor', and sat

> **His face looked like it had been stung by a thousand wasps**

Gordon with his crap leather jacket

Martin's delish dish

by a Lout!

Our dream. It was wonderful while it lasted

Back in our old jobs

down with his legs spread miles apart. He looked over to me and shouted: 'Darling, let's see what's on the menu then, shall we? I'm assuming big boy is back there doing all the cooking, yes?'

I didn't know what to say. We'd occasionally had rude customers, but I'd never known one with such anger and bad manners. When I took him the menu, I could see he had weird, sunken eyes partially covered by these strange, blonde curtains.

To be friendly, I asked him his name.

'Gordon,' he told me. 'And what's your name, sweetheart?'

'Jill,' I said.

'Fucking hell,' he snorted. 'Well, listen, "Jill", why don't you go and fetch me a pail of water, for fuck's sake. JESUS CHRIST!'

I chose to ignore his rudeness and asked him what he wanted to eat.

'Tell you what, why don't you get lover boy back there to serve up something special?'

So I went away and returned with Martin's famous sausage-and-onion pie. I proudly put it down in front of Gordon. This would put a smile on his face.

He took a mouthful and, without even swallowing the food, he shouted: 'Good Lord, this is pathetic! It tastes like

> ## 'Feel that, lover boy? A fucking disgrace!'

something I'd give my dog! Actually, I wouldn't give it to my dog. I'd give it to my mother-in-law!'

I couldn't believe what I was hearing.

Then he stood up and shoved his way past me and into the kitchen, where he stuffed the pie in Martin's face. 'Big boy, you fucking idiot, what's this crap?' he growled. 'Pie is meant to make me hard. Really solid and hard. But this has left me fucking limp,' he said. He then grabbed Martin's hand and stuffed it down the front of his tight, designer jeans.

'Feel that, lover boy? A fucking disgrace!'

I started crying. Gordon shouted at me to 'stop fucking sobbing', saying that it was 'a fucking kitchen, not a hospital ward'.

He demanded a pudding, so I gave him a chocolate dessert.

'This is actually not bad, mate,' said Gordon as he ate.

'Really?' Martin and I said in unison.

'No! It tastes like cow shit, you silly fuckers,' he shouted, and then laughed his head off, spitting food everywhere. After that, he smeared chocolate pudding all over Martin's face.

He told us we had one week to move out of the café. 'I want

to do something here,' he said. 'Maybe some kind of "authentic Chinese eating house". You know, Chinesey, Japanesey, sort of thing. But for white people. I'll call it the Lucky Cat, or some bollocks. Anyway, one week!'

He finally removed Martin's hand from inside his jeans and stormed out of the café. I remember that he pushed over tables and plates as he went. No sooner was he out on the street than he turned round and started pissing against the front window.

A little girl in the cafe started

crying and her mum covered her eyes. Gordon knocked on the window and shouted: 'One week.'

I gave Martin a hug. His face was still covered in chocolate pudding. A month later we were back in our old day jobs. Poor Martin hasn't cooked a single meal since that horrid day.

Frankenstein crossed with the Milky Bar kid

MATTHEW'S Sport & Leisure TIPS!

Whether you're wanting to shape up for the summer, try out a new activity or simply have a bit of extra-marital sex, Matthew can help you achieve your goals...

Soccer

Like most lads, I love a bit of footer. I'm a big soccer consumer and love all the legends from Madonna, to Daniel Rashford. As for my game, I'm known for my aerial dominance and silky first touch. I've been described as a cross between Liverpool legend Duncan Ferguson and my namesake, Matt La Tissier. I had a pint with La Tiss once, a top bloke with great politics for a soccer star. Sign-up today with your local five-a-side team and you'll find that footer increases stamina, improves cardiovascular health and shifts pounds faster than a virus tearing through a care home. Nice!

Climbing

Accomplished climbers like me climb with their eyes, not their bodies. You have to be able to spot a problem a mile off because otherwise, you'll land straight on your backside. It's a hobby that works multiple muscle groups, in both your upper and lower body. Plus, it means that if you ever find yourself in the shit at work, you'll be able to climb back up the greasy pole. And speaking of backsides, look at mine in that photo. Peachy!

Tug of war

Everywhere I go, people tell me I'm a 'massive tugger' and I'd have to agree. It's easy to lose breath when you are tugging but with mental strength and the right team on your side, you'll get the result you're looking for. Sometimes, when a tug reaches its natural crescendo, I like to cry out for joy. Happy tugging equals a happy ending!

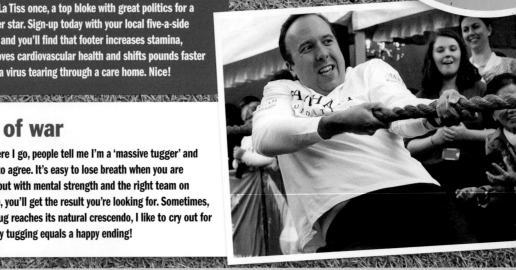

Press-Ups

Everyone loves a spunk and there's no better way of looking spunky than by having big, broad shoulders like mine. How did I achieve this level of perfection? By deploying a little known callisthenics method called the press-up. Let me explain. You begin in the prone position and then raise and lower your body using only your arms. It's natural to feel a bit bewildered when you start but give it a go and you'll soon be ripped like me. Remember to smile!

Dancing

How good am I at dancing? I'll let you be the judge of that, but it's worth noting that people often ask me whether I have any black or gay ancestors. My signature move is the 'Do the Funky Chicken' but I draw my influences from all forms of jive, from samba to ballroom and even some youthful street dance techniques such as Break Popping. So get down to your local discotheque and get busting those moves. It will improve everything from your co-ordination to your ability to attract top totty. Groovy!

Guinness

Top of the mornin' to ya, let's dress up as leprechauns, put some U2 on the jukebox and sink some of the black drink. Like every lad, I love a ruddy good pint of booze and Guinness is a great drink to help you unwind after a tough workout. The bar staff at my local love me and always make sure I get an extra special pint with VIP treatment. Cheers!

Singing

Pumping those vocal cords can help relieve tension and boost self-esteem. Looking at me, you'd be forgiven for thinking my vocal repertoire is limited to power rock anthems and other masculine musical genres like grime or hop hip. But what may surprise you is how well I can tackle more sensitive tracks. So, next time you're down your local karaoke hall, if you hear someone absolutely nailing 'Livin' On A Prayer' and then bringing everyone to tears with a delicate rendition of 'Careless Whisper', you'll know that the Mattster is in da house. Word to ya mother!

Kissing

You know how people say you should dance like no one is watching? Well, when it comes to a good snog, you should snog like everyone is watching.... on CCTV. It's important to keep lunging forward as you kiss, so your partner can't get away if she has a change of heart. Be sure to keep your hands moving across their back in a clockwise motion and moving your tongue inside her mouth anti-clockwise. I'm employing this fail-safe technique in the photo and you can see how natural I look.

The SHED of TERROR!

My next-door neighbour wasn't the nice old lady I thought she was. Not only that, my life was now in danger!
By Colin Pemberton, 36, from Devon

Me and Peter

I'd always dreamed of living in a nice peaceful village. I love people and I was drawn to being part of a tight-knit community where you could get to know everyone and all be there for one another.

So imagine how happy I was when my neighbour introduced herself, even as I was still unloading my things from the van. 'I don't know what your name is but I know what my name is – Anne,' she said.

She asked me questions about myself and, when I told her I was a nurse, she gave me a sort of knowing glance. When I said I lived alone with my cat, Peter, I heard her whisper 'definitely' under her breath. At the time, I thought nothing of it.

The next day, I was playing my Queen *Greatest Hits* CD as I unpacked and I heard her shout from the garden: 'Well, that makes sense!' I wondered what she meant.

A few days later, I bumped

Looks can be deceiving

into her again in the local village high street. She was with some friends from her church. There was an old man with medals, a sort of hardy old woman with a Union Jack scarf, and a slightly theatrical-looking young man wearing a UKIP badge. She introduced me as 'Colin, he's a confirmed bachelor'. I wasn't sure what that meant, and I was also a bit baffled when she

told me my 'acts of grave depravity' were 'intrinsically disordered'. It was all quite strange, but I just figured that she was a sweet old lady with a slightly batty, old-fashioned way of putting things.

As a nurse, I always love to help people, so when Anne asked me to help mend her shed, I was only too happy. Bless her heart, I thought, she'd even made me a cup of tea. I remember taking a few sips, then everything went dark.

When I came to, I couldn't believe what was in front of me. It was like some sort of nightmare. I don't even know how to start to describe it all.

The first thing I noticed was that I was engulfed in red light and intense heat. I could barely breathe! I was sat down, and when I tried to get up I realised that my arms and legs were strapped down. My eyes were also clamped open! It was terrifying.

> **I remember taking a few sips, then everything went dark**

There was a big machine next to me covered in flashing lights, levers and buttons. It kept spewing out puffs of black smoke.

Suddenly, this really loud classical music started playing and two large TV screens lit up in front of me. They were showing weird imagery of wars, pictures of the Pope, and Adam and Eve. Then there were images of really attractive women in flowery dresses, and a series of white families, always consisting of a husband and wife with two kids, with big thumbs-up emojis next to them. Finally, Anne's face came up on the screen smiling and blowing kisses. Then it struck me! I was trapped inside a gay conversion therapy machine inside Anne's garden shed. I had to get away! I struggled out of the straps and clamps she'd used to tie me down and burst through the flimsy wooden door. I fell to the ground exhausted. My hair was singed and I was covered in cuts and bruises but I was free – or so I thought.

Anne's chamber of horrors

A drawing of my ordeal I made in therapy

I live in London now. It's a lot noisier than I like and the people aren't as friendly but that suits me okay. I've tried reporting to the police what happened with Anne but, however much I explain it, they say she sounds like a harmless old lady.

'Don't worry about people like Anne,' they say. 'Their bark is always worse than their bite.'

I looked up and Anne was stood there on the lawn with the entire village behind her. They were all smiling with cups of tea in their hands eating pieces of cake. The medal man, the Union Jack woman and the camp boy were all there. They began to applaud and Anne whispered into my ear: 'There, don't you feel better now, Colin?'

I grabbed Peter the cat and ran off as fast as I could. Dusk was turning into night-time as I sprinted breathlessly through the woods. Anne and her mob began chasing me, carrying burning torches and howling as they ran.

Carrying burning torches and howling as they ran

They were all much older than me and the cake was obviously giving them cramp, but they were fast and seemed to have superhuman stamina. Eventually, I managed to outrun them and made it to a small country lane. I stood at the side of the road and tried to hitch a lift.

A man on a motorbike pulled over.

He was dressed head to toe in leather, with a handkerchief sticking out of his back pocket, and he had a huge handlebar moustache on his face. 'Hop on board,' he said. I didn't need to be asked twice.

As we sped away, I turned to see Anne and her friends, all collapsed on the ground, staring at me. Even though I was safe, the sight of them sent a chill down my spine.

Me now on Hampstead Heath

ANIMAL world

Every week, *Have A Wank* features a different story about mankind's love for animals. This week, lizard enthusiast David from the Isle of Wight tells us about the joy of owning mini-reptiles.

Look at this cutey

People sometimes say to me that only weirdos like lizards. I always reply: 'Listen, pal, owning pets like cats and dogs is what you've been conditioned to do. So who's the weirdo now?'

Whether it's a bearded dragon, gecko or a blue-tongued skink, lizards will quickly become your best friend. They are calm, easy to handle and you'll never have to take them for a walk in the rain like the zombies in your local park.

Lizards can be loving and affectionate companions who will keep you company even when everyone else turns against you and you become a figure of national ridicule. You don't need to buy huge tins of food for them – like students from north London, they can survive on a diet of kale and bugs.

They say a dog is like its owner, but they only say that because they've been carefully conditioned from the womb to think so. Man's best friend isn't a dog, it's a lizard, and it's literally insane to think otherwise.

And I think by now it's obvious that dog festivals like Cruft's are just opportunities for corporations to gather your data. Wake up, sheeple!

You wouldn't catch lizard owners out that easily. That said, owning lizards doesn't come without its challenges. They can be bossy and sneaky little so-and-sos. I sometimes joke that I don't know if I'm in charge of the lizards or the lizards are in charge of me!

Recently, I've started monetising my hobby by writing fantastical lizard-inspired storybooks and taking my pet reptiles to kids' birthday parties. They love it when I show them all the different scaly pets I've got, and we always have a good sing-along to 'Puff the Magic Dragon' and the theme tune from the original *Godzilla*.

I tell the kids all about the lizards and I usually try and leave them with some deeper messages about life too. It's important to open kids' eyes before they get too brainwashed. (Actually, I think the fact that lizards can't close their eyes is one of the things that draws me to them.)

I hope I've convinced you that you should follow in my footsteps and delve into this wonderful, scaly world. If you need any more information, just send me an email (but not via a 5G connection).

What are you waiting for? Get down to your local pet shop and buy yourself some reptiles. Lizards rule!

LIZARD FACT FILE

- There are more than **6,000** different **lizard** species. (Makes you think, doesn't it?)
- They can live **anywhere**. (Bit worrying.)
- They are **cold-blooded**. (Erm, hello?)
- They can detach their own tails if they need to. (One question: why?)
- Many of them can **change colour** and other aspects of their appearances. (Are you thinking what we're thinking?)

There's something shifty about this one

Win! A TRIP TO BARNARD CASTLE

Escape to Durham

COMPETITION CROSSWORD!

Don't miss your chance to win this incredible trip of a lifetime to the wonderful market town of Barnard Castle.

This four-day package includes:

One course lunch at the renowned Durham Services. A tour of the historic market town with plenty of time for souvenir shopping and virus spreading. An eyesight test at picturesque beauty spot Houghall Woods. Sponsored by Specshoppers. 3-star accommodation at the famous Cummings residence.**

Your trip is guaranteed and will not be affected by pandemic outbreaks or government intervention.

*Breakfast, Lunch, Dinner, Towels, Bedding and Soap not provided.

*Check out 6am.

Durham services

Crossword grid: 7 Across starts with V I S I O N

Across

7 Something you test with a long drive on public roads (6)

8 Route via somewhere unnecessary to go (6)

9 Sight-based game, great for car trips (1-3)

10 State of isolation or restricted movement (8)

11 Long trip, typically forbidden during lockdown (7)

13 Castle water barriers (5)

15 Most suitable, as in 'this is the ___ place to test my eyesight' (5)

17 Something you wear to fix your eyesight (7)

20 Not correct, as in 'this policy is ___ ' (8)

21 Perceives ocularly (4)

22 Check, as in 'I must ___ my eyesight' (6)

23 People running the government; circus performers (6)

Down

1 Ludicrous failure, as in 'this policy is a ___' (6)

2 Skilled at deceit (4)

3 'Come ___ ', to end in failure (7)

4 Official decree that applies to everyone (5)

5 Spending a lot of time preparing (8)

6 Deceive another by being oh-so very smart (6)

12 Totally necessary lockdown adventure to Barnard Castle, e.g. (4,4)

14 Medical facilities that normal people use to test eyesight etc. (7)

16 Explanation for trip to Barnard Castle, e.g.; nonsense (6)

18 Looking closely and with interest (6)

19 Gives permission for (5)

21 See something that you're looking for (4)

Britain's Most HAUNTED TESCO!

Renowned paranormal expert Margaret Peters investigates the strange racist ghost tormenting customers and staff at Tesco Express, Windsor.

When you head to the supermarket for your weekly shop, there are lots of things you want: meat and two veg, 20 embassy lights, a bottle of Yop and some strong white rum.

One thing you don't want is to be abused by a racist ghost. But that's exactly what seems to have been happening to the good people of Windsor in the aisles of their local Tesco Express.

It was the store's manager, Vipal, who first got in touch with me about the problem. 'Margaret,' he said. 'As the UK's number one and most respected paranormal expert, can you come and investigate what's going on at our store?'

I was only too happy to oblige, and before long I too was engulfed in this paranormal puzzle.

My journey began when I met the store's most longstanding customer, Marjorie Jacobs. Here's what she told me:

'I'd only nipped out to get a few bits for our tea. My John loves his Friday night curry, you see? I'd loaded up the trolley with some Tesco Value chicken fillets, a few cans of Fosters and some wet wipes, just to be on the safe side. Then I headed

> **'You want to watch it eating that foreign muck'**

An unlikely spot for a haunting

over to the World Food aisle and that's when things started going a bit weird.'

'The moment I picked up the Korma Paste, this strange ghostly figure appeared and sidled up right next to me. I froze on the spot. He leant into my ear and whispered: "You want to watch it eating that foreign muck, that lot still throw spears at each other."'

She told me he then floated away, shouting things about 'blacks'. What an ordeal!

I got a similar story from Fenella, a local estate agent who was planning a Chinese meal to celebrate a friend's birthday. 'I was trying to decide between Sweet and Sour or Chicken Chow Mein sauce,'

Face of the monster

Sharwood's COOKING SAUCE KORMA

Too spicy for him?

so upset.

'I know I've got a bit of facial hair, but I've never been mistaken for a man before. When I told Gary, my boyfriend, he was livid and he immediately agreed to take me away to Centre Parcs for the weekend to help me get over it.'

As if what this sniping spectre gets up to during opening hours wasn't shocking enough, when I heard what happens when the store closes at night, a paranormal chill went through my whole body.

Meet Chris. He's one of the guys responsible for keeping those supermarket shelves stocked with all the goodies that you love. He works in the dead of night when the store is closed to the general public.

One evening, he was stacking the shelves as per usual but, when he got to the World Food section, things 'got a little freaky.'

'I was walking away having just finished stacking the Uncle Ben's rice shelf, when all of a sudden I hear this crash. I turn round and I see boxes and jars flying through the air and smashing on the floor. Sauce, rice, poppadums, you name it; everything scattered all over the aisle. The place was an absolute mess.'

But what Chris told me next was a real metaphysical mystery – even to an old-time pro like me. He explained that the bigoted spectre never ever damaged the hummus, taramasalata, olives or pita bread. 'Basically, Greek food would always stay where it was,' he said. 'Funny that.'

A paranormal chill went through my whole body

Margaret's EXPERT verdict:

No shopper deserves to be harassed as they are choosing what to eat for their dinner, but this ghastly ghoul clearly doesn't care a jot about people's feelings. Not only does he intimidate the customers, but he also smashes the stock and airs views that are a little out of sync with modern Britain.

My hunch is that whatever life this man lived before passing over, he wasn't a very nice person. Just my opinion, of course.

she told me. 'As I reached for the jar of Sharwood's, I felt the presence of an otherworldly being peering over my left shoulder.' Terrifying stuff! 'I'm Philip,' he told her. 'Don't tell anyone but I've heard that everyone who eats that Oriental food gets slitty eyes.'

She says she saw him again when she was browsing the sanitary towels and that he started ranting about how women 'make a bloody mess out of everything' and then checked with her: 'You are a woman, aren't you?' Poor Fenella says she's never been

All DOLLED UP!

Being undermined by my wife time and time again left me lonely and isolated. Then I found true love in the most unexpected way.

By Nigel, 57, from Kent.

Since childhood, I've been trying to get the world to notice me. My mother would always say, 'If you want people to like you Nigel then stop talking so much!' I hated that, and I never listened. Over time I proved her wrong and climbed my way up society's social ladder. The problem was that every time I'd be on the verge of getting respect something went wrong.

Take my work. I'd been so close to getting a seat with the big boys. I'd put in the hours, made my mark and been a total cunt for years. But people just seemed to lose interest in me once I had achieved something. It was very painful and I would often find myself crying as I made the long drive back to Kent from London.

I got precious little support at home. My wife, Kirsten, would continually ridicule me and say things like, 'You'd have more friends if you just kept your right-wing views to yourself, Nigel.' She had a terrible habit of undermining me in a way that only a woman can. Don't pretend you don't know what I mean.

She loved making fun of me in front of our friends too, particularly when we met them at the local pub for quiz night. I hated the way she'd get all the questions right then rub my face in it. So what if I could only answer the ones about World War Two? She thought she was so much more clever than me.

I knew it was time to take back

Love of my life - Eva

My favourite magazine

control of my life. One day, while I was browsing my favourite Nazi-memorabilia magazine, *Reich Relics Monthly*, an advert near the back caught my eye. It read: 'Do you desire a woman that never answers back and is ready to satisfy her man – 24/7?' I carried on reading and was soon absolutely tenting my tweed.

The ad was offering 'life-like silicon Nazi sex dolls for only £1200'. I was mesmerized at the thought of such an erotic encounter, and the fact that I wouldn't actually be sleeping with a real human being meant that Kirsten couldn't accuse me of adultery. It was perfect!

I couldn't log onto PayPal quickly enough and I actually screamed with joy when I got the dispatch email telling me my doll was on its way.

When she arrived, I quickly hid her in the disused World War Two bunker at the end of our garden. Kirsten hated going in there so I knew she would never find her. That night I waited until Kirsten was fast asleep before I crept out to meet my new lover. It was exhilarating, I felt like an undercover operative behind enemy lines. I peeled back the layers of bubble wrap and revealed the most beautiful perfect face peering up at me. She seemed so calm and, most importantly, didn't say a word. She was dressed head to toe in titillating Nazi regalia, including a very believable bright red swastika armband. I was so aroused that I climaxed immediately in my pants.

Over the next few weeks, I began making two or three trips a night down to the bunker to meet my sweetheart. I called her Eva and each sexual rendezvous seemed more passionate than the last. We were so alive! It didn't just feel like I was making love to some fascist totty; it felt like I was

Kirsten never took me seriously

> **Each sexual rendezvous seemed more passionate than the last**

making love to history itself, rogering my way back to the 1930s.

Before long I was so desperate for nationalistic nooky that I was slipping out to the bunker during the day too. I couldn't help myself. But as usual in my life, when things are going well, heartache is right around the corner.

Kirsten had gone shopping with her friend Sue, and so I decided to spend the afternoon in Eva's company. We were deep in the throes of unbridled passion when the bunker door swung open. Kirsten and Sue had come home early and caught us in the act.

At first, I thought Kirsten would be livid, but she just started laughing and told Sue to take a photo of me. Before I could demand that she delete the photo, it had been shared on their girls' WhatsApp group. Typical Kirsten!

I now live in the bunker full-time – my own independent kingdom. For a while, I tried joining the pub quiz remotely, via Zoom. But every time I tried to answer a question, people laughed and called me silly names, like 'Nazi-Nigel', 'Dick-tator' and 'Swas-dicker'.

Well, the joke is on them because every sneer pulls Eva and I closer together. I've finally met someone that shows me the respect I deserve and no amount of name-calling can take that away.

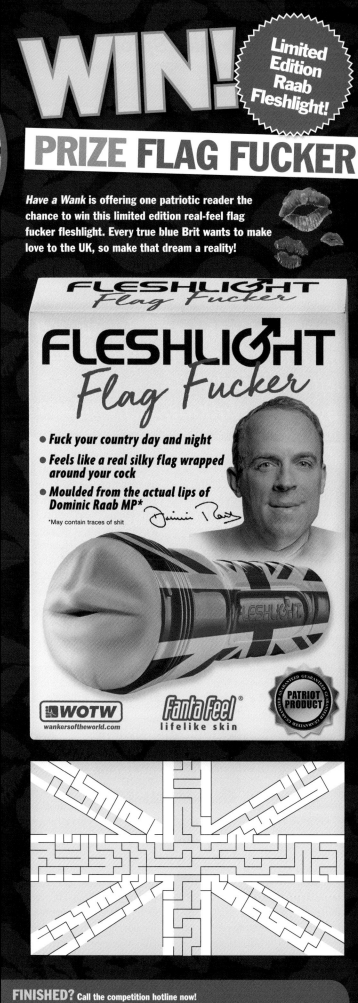

MY HORRIBLE RACIST BABY!

I thought having a child would make me happy, but the reality of parenthood left me devastated.

By Karen Watkins, 32, from Luton

Baby David

Wrapped up in his fluffy cotton blanket he looked up at me with those big, blue eyes. My little baby David couldn't have been more perfect. I'd just become a mum and I finally felt like my life had some meaning.

It had all started when my ex-boyfriend, Dave, got me up the duff in the car park behind Luton bowling alley. He always kept a Saint George's flag tucked behind the bins that he would unfold and lay down on the ground like a duvet. He called it his 'British bulldog shag towel'.

He gave me a proper good seeing to that afternoon and then bought me a tropical fruit burst Slush Puppy afterwards as a 'well done'. It just seemed like a bit of fun but, a few months later, I got this excruciating pain in my stomach. It wouldn't go away but I thought it must just be the dreaded bubble guts I'd sometimes get after a heavy night out on the WKDs.

But when my turd came out all solid and perfectly formed with a clean, tidy pinch, I knew something must be up. I bought a pregnancy test straight away and pissed on it. I looked down and shouted: 'OMG! I'm having a baby!' I called Dave right away to tell him the good news, but he told me to 'fuck right off' so I decided to go it alone.

Nine months later, I gave birth to a lovely bouncing baby boy and decided to name him David, after his dad. He was the sweetest little thing in the world, always smiling and giggling, and so easy to look after. I was the happiest girl in Luton and everything was just great, or so I thought.

After a couple of months, I realised that he wasn't growing any hair on the top of his head, only on the sides. He also seemed to have a problem with his eyesight. I took him to my GP – the lovely Doctor Mehdi. He examined little David and said that he was permanently bald on top and that he would also need glasses. I was

> **'Nothing important has been written in Arabic for five hundred years!'**

devastated, but what happened next blew my world apart.

Dr Mehdi was smiling at David and making funny little faces at him when, suddenly, my baby boy opened his mouth really wide, paused for a second, then started talking. I couldn't believe what I was seeing – he was only a few months old but there he was forming proper sentences. It was a real-life miracle! I started welling up. I remember thinking how well-spoken his accent was. My little cherub not only talked but talked proper posh!

My joy soon turned to despair, though, when I realised what he was actually saying. 'Listen to me, Dr Ahmed, or whatever your damn name is. Nothing important has been written in Arabic for five hundred years!' he sneered.

I'll never forget those horrible first words or the look on poor Dr Mehdi's face. From that day forward, David didn't shut up and, whenever we'd go out, he'd want a debate with some random stranger about race and what he called the 'Culture War' or some bollocks.

One afternoon when I was pushing him up Luton high street, there were some teenagers sat on a wall smoking a spliff and listening to music. David jumped out of the buggy and crawled towards them. Before I could react, he was screaming abuse at them.

'This is the problem with Britain today!' he shrieked. 'Look at you! All of you are white yet you dress like you are black and listen to this bloody black music. This Jamaican patois that's intruded England is why so many of us have this sense of living in literally a foreign country. The whites have become black: a particular sort of violent, destructive, nihilistic, gangster culture.'

The teenagers were as shocked as I was, and I remember that the youngest one in the group, who had his cap on backwards, started crying. My little David was only eight months old, but I already felt like I'd lost him.

There is a bandstand in the middle of the high street and David made a beeline towards it, so he could address everyone.

'People need to stop going on about slavery,' he shouted. 'It was abolished in 1833 for crying out loud! Slavery was not genocide, otherwise, there wouldn't be so many damn blacks in Africa or in Britain would there?'

I rushed home in floods of

Keiss Castle

Me Now

Me and baby David

tears. Around that same time, he insisted on being called Dr David and started wearing little tweed jackets and stripy shirts. He also threw away the NHS glasses I'd got from the doctor and replaced them with these round tortoiseshell patterned ones, which made him look like even more of a cunt.

I knew that something had to be done. The one thing that little David still relied on and couldn't live without was the milk from my bosoms. It was his greatest weakness

and, no matter how far he travelled across the country, speaking in public against Muslims or blacks, he would always come crawling back for a suckle on Mummy's teat.

So I packed some bags and travelled to the furthest place I could get to in the UK – a place called John o' Groats. My boobs were full of that warm nectar I knew little David still craved so much. I found my way to some old ruins called Keiss Castle, flopped out my bulging bosom onto a rocky crag, and waited. Days and days passed, the wind howling through the ruins.

Then, one rainy night as I lay waiting, I heard the patter of tiny footsteps making their way up the spiral staircase. Suddenly, David's silhouette appeared in a doorway, his eyes full of tears. He looked weak and pasty.

'Please, Mummy, let me have

> **'Slavery was not genocide, otherwise, there wouldn't be so many damn blacks in Africa'**

a sip, I'm so, so hungry. Just one sip, oh, please.'

As he lunged towards my chest, I saw my chance. I grabbed his pudgy body and flipped him around, his head now poking out through the slitted window of the castle. I yanked his little corduroy trousers down around his ankles, held him firmly, then spanked his bare arse red raw.

As I sat there pummelling his tiny body, the waves crashed against the castle walls below and I knew one thing for certain: no one could hear little David crying for help.

Dear Karen

Is your name Karen? Do you spend your life feeling distinctly unimpressed by other people's behaviour? Well help is at hand! Let our agony aunt, Karen McGreggor help you navigate the hardships of modern life.

Karen from Basingstoke writes:

The other day, I saw a man in our close I've never seen before. He had brown skin, so naturally, I approached him to find out what he was up to.

He told me he was a delivery driver for a company called 'Deliveryoo' or something, and that he was dropping off some food to one of our neighbours. A likely story! He must've been a professional criminal because he had even painted a 'Deliveryoo' logo on his jacket to try and back up this obvious lie. I didn't come down with the last shower, I told him.

I was particularly worried about his giant square backpack. He could have been hiding anything in there: a jihad bomb, or even a child refugee. He opened it and took out a pizza, but again, I knew this was all part of his scam.

Luckily, I filmed the whole encounter on my smartphone and uploaded it to my neighbourhood watch Facebook group so other Karens are aware of this shady character. Did I do the right thing?

Karen says: You did the right thing, Karen. You can't be too careful these days and you're perfectly entitled to stand up to someone acting so suspiciously. He'll think twice about coming back to your little close now! Well done you.

Narrow minded!

Karen from Cheshire writes:

Our favourite fish and chip restaurant is closed for refurbishments, so my husband Peter and I decided to try a new oriental restaurant on the high street called The Wagamama.

We felt quite special as we were ushered to our table and we both ordered our favourite dish when we eat foreign – omelette and chips. But our jaws dropped when the waiter, who looked like he was still at school, told us that they didn't serve omelettes.

I told him that the other Chinese in the area – Mr Chan's – does a perfectly good omelette and chips, so if one oriental restaurant can do it, why can't they? It simply defies all logic.

I demanded to speak with the manager and I gave him a real piece of my mind.

Other customers started filming and sharing it online. Now I'm getting hate mail. What should I do next?

Karen says: I can't believe how disgustingly they treated you, Karen. What is this country coming to? Keep every letter and message that's sent to you because some people are going to lose their jobs over this. Make sure you film the postman who delivers the letters too. He won't be doing that round much longer!

Scam artist

Life's little luxuries

Demand an apology

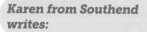

Face nappy

I would recommend sending a stern email to the salon, copying in your local MP and trading standards office. The very least Babs can do is offer you an apology and a year's free treatments!

Karen from Southend writes:

I've been going to the same hairdressers now for over 20 years, but I was shocked to find out recently that they've hired a coloured lady as a stylist.

Ask anyone, and they'll tell you I'm the least racist person you'll ever meet, but I'm afraid I'm not comfortable with having my hair cut by someone from a different racial background. I simply can't see how she would know how to cut a white woman's hair properly. And I'm sure a coloured person wouldn't want a white person cutting their frizzy afro hair. How would that even work?

I've known Babs – the owner – for years, so I called her over and explained my predicament. You won't believe what happened next. She threw me out and called me racist! I've never been so insulted. Well, you should've seen their faces when I told them that my cousin Tina is married to a black man. It was priceless! I knew I'd won, so I walked out with my head held high.

I'd appreciate your support, Karen.

Karen says: You have my full support, Karen. We all need our 'happy place' and it's literally criminal that yours has been tarnished in this way.

Karen from Orpington writes:

I recently visited my dad in hospital and, as I arrived at his emphysema ward, I was appalled to be approached by a member of staff and asked why I wasn't wearing a Covid mask.

Can you believe the cheek of it? I said if I want to take a risk, then that's my business, but this 'doctor' told me that we don't wear a mask to protect ourselves – it's to protect others. The thickest thing I've ever heard in my life.

I won't wear a face nappy for anyone. This country is sleepwalking to disaster if we continue to over-react to this virus, which is little more than a cold for 99.8 per cent of people who get it.

Karen says: I think this 'doctor' must be a doctor of stupidity! How dare he ask you to wear a mask? Karen, you are right to be wary of this whole 'virus' narrative. In fact, if you go online and do your own research, some experts believe that this pandemic is a massive scam cooked up by Bill Gates and China to sell face masks and inject us with 5G microchips.

Karen from Langley writes:

As every Karen knows, there is nothing worse than when your bunions are playing up. I often have flare-ups and, while I'm the last one to complain, I do reserve the right to use the disabled parking at my local Asda. If bunions aren't a disability, then I don't know what is.

But the other day, I was disgusted when I was approached by a foreign woman who told me her husband is 'actually disabled' and that I need a blue badge to park in the disabled bay. The cheek!

As you can imagine, the red mist descended quickly. I kept telling her that she didn't know the rules in this country and that, if she didn't like it, then she knew what she could do.

I stood my ground – even though it made my bunions worse – and after a while, she and her husband drove off. I noticed her husband was in tears. If I was married to a trout like that, I would be too!

Karen says: It's awful when tolerant people like you and I have our good will trampled on, but I'm glad that you didn't back down. As long as we decent people stand up for ourselves, then, one by one, we will prevail!

Bunions – a true disability!

USED and ABUSED!

Our fight to save our brother from his evil tormentor nearly killed us.
Janet, 55, from the USA

Uri and Michael

They say first impressions count, but my first impression of one man couldn't have been more wrong – and my family almost paid the hardest price for it.

I'll never forget the first time we met Uri. We were at the palace of my brother Michael's best friend, Mohamed. Mo introduced Uri as his 'magical friend from Israel', and everyone agreed that he was really cool and mystical. He did amazing tricks and told us about the special powers he loved to use.

He said he once even changed the course of a 1996 soccer match between England and Scotland by moving the soccer ball off the penalty spot with just the power of his mind!

We didn't have a clue what he was going on about, but we all thought it was fantastic anyway, especially Michael. Overnight he and Uri became best buddies.

Soon enough Uri moved in with Michael and that's when things started to turn nasty. One day, I went around to the house and to my horror Uri had dressed Michael up as Peter Pan and strapped him into a theatrical flying harness. He and his mates had spent the whole day flying Michael about and laughing at him. That sucked.

Another time, I caught Uri snapping all of Michael's spoons. Not only that – he was wearing Michael's favourite red leather jacket and white glove. I asked him where Michael was. He just laughed and said: 'Ask me no questions, I tell you no lies.'

I searched for Michael for hours and eventually found him in a secret padded room, surrounded by video cameras. Uri had dressed him up in some ET pyjamas and hidden his wig, so he was completely bald. He

had his hands tied behind his back and Uri had given him a pink candyfloss beard. Michael said that he didn't mind, but I know my brother – I could see he was upset.

Ask me no questions I tell you no lies

The time had come to call in my other brothers: Jackie, Tito, Jermaine, Marlon and Randy. We joined forces and drove to Michael's house, determined to remove Uri forever. 'That guy is history,' said Randy.

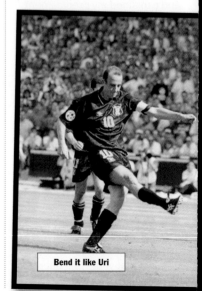

Bend it like Uri

Me with Michael and Uri the tormentor

My cool brothers

No sooner had we arrived than we saw through one of the rear windows that Uri now had dressed Michael up as a scarecrow. Even worse, he was force-feeding him candy from Michael's favourite clown candy fountain. It was a devastating sight to see. We knocked on the door but Uri wouldn't answer.

Tito said we should break in through Michael's skylight. We crept onto the roof and my five brothers created a human chain, so they could lower themselves into the amusement-arcade dinosaur room.

As we descended, Randy let go of the chain too early and bounced off the T-Rex merry-go-round but, fortunately, landed perfectly on his rhinestone platform shoes. Then he started break-dancing.

'Randy!' I screamed. 'Remember, we're here to save Michael!'

We crept downstairs and made our way through the marshmallow playroom into where Uri was tormenting our brother.

There he was – still bald, dressed like a scarecrow and with mascara running down his beautiful, white cheeks. His face lit up when he saw us creeping behind Uri, and that gave the game away.

There was no time to waste – Jermaine, Jackie and Tito pulled Uri by his tinted, blow-dried hair and dragged that man's sorry ass into Michael's secret soundproofed room.

They left the door open so I could hear what was going on. They beat on his ass like it was the 1970s. I've never heard a grown man cry quite like it. It sounded like a sea lion was caught in a fishing net. 'Haven't I suffered enough?'

he kept yelping.

Afterwards, Uri was still crying his eyes out but, between sobs, he told us all his powers were a lie. 'I had nothing to do with that penalty kick,' he told us. 'I bend the spoons before my performances and then switch them when people are distracted!'

The crazy-ass fool was begging to go home but we tossed him into Michael's porcelain clown room for the night and listened to him scream as we ate ice cream and high-fived one another.

It was awesome to see Michael looking so happy. He even did some dancing for us. I

tried to put his wig back on him, but he just poured Pepsi-Cola over his head and giggled.

It was great to be all together. Michael encouraged the rest of my brothers to join in with him as he danced and sang. As one of the songs reached its crescendo, all these little white children with blonde hair and sweet faces suddenly appeared from the cupboards.

The lord only knows how they got there, but they also started dancing. It was all such fun. Uri had gone and we were loving life again. We'd all had enough of the weirdness.

> **I tried to put his wig back on him, but he just poured Pepsi-Cola over his head and giggled**

Taking the
Perfect Shit
with *Mary Berry*

Mary is best known as the star of television's Great British Bake Off but, when she's not baking a chocolate sponge, there's nothing she likes more than squeezing out a fat, steaming turd. Let the queen of cake take you through her fail-safe technique

Choose the right cubicle

Floor-to-ceiling doors are essential. I don't really want people to be able to see my knickers around my ankles and I certainly don't want Paul Hollywood's face appearing under the cubicle door again.

Acoustics are important too. You want to make the most of your every fart, heave and splatter. Sometimes I like to record them on my phone for posterity. They don't call it the thunder box for nothing, so make sure your toilet has great echo facilities.

Toilet-roll position

If you fail to prepare, then you prepare to fail, and there's nothing worse than realising too late that the toilet paper isn't close to hand and that you're going to have to perform that shameful, tightly clenched hobble across the bathroom floor. Avoid this common mistake by ensuring the loo roll is no more than 25 inches away.

Use a landing bay

Before you sit down, lay some paper in the bowl to avoid splashback. Taking a shit should be the highlight of your day, so don't let a giant splash of murky toilet water up your Jacksie spoil it.

Have your cake and excrete it

Different cakes produce different results when they come out of the other end. A dry rock cake is going to block you up and belatedly produce a succession of currants, raisins and blueberries, which will carpet bomb the toilet like something out of a World War II movie. I find that anything with a silky buttercream pudding produces an excellent consistency on release.

Ghost shit

We all have our favourite genre of poo. Some people like a good honest log, others prefer a more of a splatter. (I have to say, I find those in the latter camp a bit suspicious.) My favourite is undoubtedly the ghost shit, where it comes out so perfectly that there's nothing to wipe away and nothing in the lavatory bowl. Spooky!

Toilet roll etiquette

Some people have their lavatory roll facing inwards, others prefer it facing outwards. It's just another of society's culture wars. For me, only an uneducated reprobate would choose to have the paper facing inwards. Animals.

A good read

Having something good to read really helps me relax into a good flow. I find *Bravo Two Zero* by Andy McNab usually does the trick. The story of the SAS patrol's battles behind enemy lines really mirrors the struggles one encounters when defecating. And the SAS motto applies in both scenarios too: Who Dares Wins.

It ain't over till it's over

I learned this tip from my great-aunt Maud. 'Mary,' she would say as I sat watching her piping one out each morning. 'Never pinch the loaf too early dear.' And she was right. When you've got a busy day ahead, it's tempting to use that sphincter to pinch out at just 80% of the loaf. But you'll only be setting yourself up for trouble down the line. It's very hard to achieve the same muscular leverage over the remaining 20% at a later date. You'll most likely end up heaving and pushing so hard you'll put your lower back out.

BRITAIN'S
Most Punchable
FACE!

Over the past year, our readers have been sending in pictures of their other halves as we search for the man with Britain's most punchable face.

1st Place

Michael our winner!

Win a limited edition mug!

Have a Wank BRITAIN'S Most Punch-able FACE!

We've been inundated with entries and our electronic postbag has absolutely bulged with photographs of the ghastliest-looking people.

The standard has been astonishingly high, but one entrant stood out and literally took the judges' breath away. Sarah from London sent in a picture of her ex-husband, Michael, and we could hardly believe what we were seeing.

Where to start? Michael's beady, goggly eyes reminded us of the classic hateable TV puppet, Pob. We found his bulbous little cheeks fantastically annoying and his moist fish lips turned our stomachs in a way no other entrant managed. His permanent expression of mild surprise was also cited.

One judge described the moment they first set sight on him. 'He looked like an overgrown smarmy brat who has just been told they've got top marks in an exam. It's no exaggeration to say I immediately wanted to pummel his stupid face, right from the very first glimpse of him.'

Another panel member explained that they had to go straight to the gym after seeing the picture. 'I thought the speed bag would be enough to take the itch away. But ultimately I had to have a full session on the heavy bag before I could start to feel normal again.'

Sarah also sent in some videos of Michael talking and it was these that swung the judges. 'His cunty little voice and snake-like persona absolutely bowled us over.'

'We weren't at all surprised when Sarah told us that she and Michael had 'drifted apart over the past couple of years.' If we had to wake up next to that face, we'd have flung ourselves off the top of Big Ben years ago.

Michael told us: 'When I found out I had won, I was over the moon. Coming second would have been a slap in the face, so I'm proud to have managed such a walloping win. If only the haters could see me now. Thank you, *Have A Wank!*'

Sarah with her ex husband – our winner, Michael

Expert's view: what makes a face punchable?

There are several standout features on fist-able faces:

Wet lips: When someone looks like they spend their day dribbling and licking their own lips, it's enough to turn a saint into a psychopath.

Smugness: People who are pleased with themselves are annoying but faces that are pleased with themselves take our rage levels to new heights.

Annoying smiles: Some people's smiles make you want to marry them, other people's smiles make you want to murder them. A particular offender is the perma-smile of someone who grins 24 hours a day. Fuck off!

Pummel pleasure

Life Of A Hero Up In SMOKE!

Catching my little boy taking drugs was a devastating blow, but what happened next broke my heart.

Sarah Jenkins, 47, from Peterborough

Jason defiled national hero

Me now with no Amazon

I knew there was something funny going on when I heard that reggae music coming from my son's bedroom. I've got nothing against black people or their music – in fact, some of my favourite singers are black – but when I can hear it blasting from down the end of the garden, a line has been crossed.

To be honest, I don't know where it all went wrong for my Jason. He was always such a lovely sweet boy. When he was small, he'd dress up as a soldier and it made me so proud to see my little lad in British uniform.

I tell you who else was proud: his granddad, God rest his soul. He'd flown a Spitfire during the war and was a real hero. They don't make men like that anymore. I remember him crying tears of joy as he watched Jason marching up and down our close shouting 'no surrender'. Those were his first words.

So imagine my shock when I heard Jamaican music blasting from his bedroom. 'Not under my roof, thank you!' I started to run upstairs, determined to give him a piece of my mind. I was halfway up when a weird stench suddenly hit me. I wasn't sure what the smell was at first. We'd been having some issues with the new neighbours in the area cooking their smelly spicy meals, so I just assumed it must be that. But as I got closer to Jason's door the smell became

> **A weird stench suddenly hit me**

more and more intense.

I burst into the room and immediately realised what was going on: my boy was taking drugs! 'What are you doing Jason?!' I shouted. His eyes were red and his face looked pale. 'It's just a bit of weed, Mum. Chill out.' The room was so thick with smoke I could hardly breathe. I was angry and terrified. I snatched the pipe out of his hand and that's when my day went from bad to worse. The evil smoking contraption

Little Jason made us all so proud

that's when Jason finally opened up. He said he'd bought it on the internet from Amazon. I immediately went online and wrote to the owner of the shop, a man called Jeff Bezos. I told him he should be ashamed, selling such things. Helping kids to take drugs is one thing – to be fair, I can get through a family-sized pack of Nytol on a bad day. But dragging a national

that I wouldn't be shopping at Amazon anymore. 'Shop local, shop British!' I shouted, as I deleted the app from my phone. It felt great. 'See how long you survive now, Mr Bezos,' I thought and laughed out loud.

For weeks afterwards, though, I kept looking out of the front window and wondering why no one was coming to see me anymore. Had I been

cancelled too? Life was hard without my daily dose of brown packages being handed over by a swarthy delivery boy. Those interactions would always give me a little lift and make me feel like someone out there loved me.

Jeff Bezos should be ashamed

I even had to start going into real-life shops again which has been tough what with there being so many different nationalities out there now. You wouldn't even know you're in Peterborough half the time. Don't get me wrong, I like a bit of variety, but hearing all those foreign languages makes me nervous. Always feels like they're talking about you, know what I mean?

Anyway, I'm sticking to my guns and I will not be bowed. If Tom Moore can walk up and down his garden, I can keep boycotting Amazon. So, like my old granddad and Captain Tom, I'm going to be brave. Stick that in your pipe and smoke it!

What happened to my sweet boy?

was shaped like the face of Captain Tom Moore. It made me sick to my stomach to see such an incredible British man defiled. I don't believe in coronavirus, but what he achieved was nothing short of breathtaking. Walking 100 lengths of his back garden and co-recording a song with Michael Ball – incredible!

Well, I thought, we didn't leave the EU for things like this to go on! I grabbed Jason around the neck and demanded to know where he had bought it from. He refused to answer so I said: 'I bet it was that weird new foreign shop on the high street with the wigs in the window.'

I told him I was going to give them a piece of my mind and

hero into it is disgraceful.

I opened my Amazon app and found the product: it was called a Captain Tom Ceramic Bong. Then I tried a few searches to investigate what other disgusting products were on sale. I discovered a shocking trail of horrific items: Black Lives Matter pencil cases, Gay Pride T-shirts, books about Gareth Southgate and, worst of all, German wine.

And wait till you hear this: they were selling 20 different Elton John CDs but only one from Lawrence Fox. There's nothing I hate more than this modern-day cancel culture!

I decided there and then

Captain Tom Ceramic Bong Pipe
★★☆☆☆ 15
Hero of War COVID Ceramic Bong, Bong Pipe Water Bong for Smoking Bong Bowl 250mm Height Easy to Carry

MADE IN CHINA

Price: £29.99 ✓prime
FREE delivery: Saturday, Feb 13
Order within 2 hrs 53 mins Details

Can you believe it!

Dear Des
UNBREAKABLE Bond of Friendship

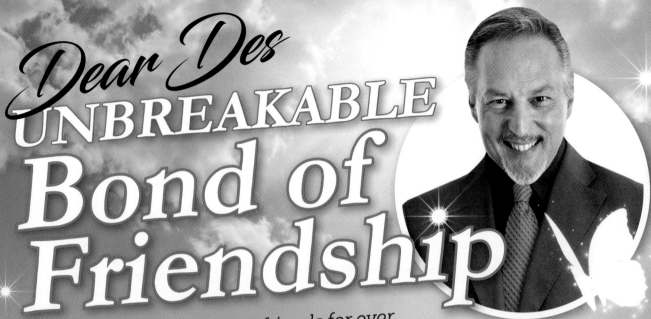

Jimmy and Margaret were friends for over 30 years... now they are together forever.

I've had people writing to me for many years now asking to make contact with loved ones in the afterlife, but I can honestly say that I've never been as moved as I was when I read this incredible letter from Mark. Sit back and enjoy, readers.

Dear Des,

Next April it will be 10 years since my beautiful mother Margaret passed away. Known affectionately as 'Maggie' by those that loved her, she was a tough woman who was never afraid to speak her mind. But when I think back to her happiest memories, they were undoubtedly spent with her dearest and best friend, Jimmy.

They were inseparable and absolutely loved each other's company. Jimmy always made Mum giggle with his eccentric dress sense and funny little stories about his life. They'd be up until the wee hours some nights chatting away and howling with laughter as Jimmy shared stories about his time as a pop DJ or his nights having sex with dead bodies in Broadmoor Hospital. 'He really is a card,' Mum would say after a night spent knocking back the whiskies with Jim.

Their relationship was a real two-way street. Jimmy would be just as happy to sit back and let Mum be the one reciting the amusing anecdotes. He especially loved her stories about the naughty tricks she liked to play on the poor people who lived in our town. I'll never forget those tears of joy streaming down their faces.

It was such fun for me as a young lad being allowed to stay up late sometimes and join in the fun. 'Go and sit on Uncle Jimmy's knee,' Mum would bark. He would pretend I was a cowboy and he was the horse, then jiggle me up and down. It was really hard to stay perched on his lap because he always wore these shiny tracksuits that would make you slip off. He also had this incredible magic trick where he could tickle your bottom without using his hands. He was a real showman.

> **'Go and sit on Uncle Jimmy's knee'**

Needless to say that when Jimmy got himself into a spot of bother, Mum would be there to help out, and vice versa. I remember the local police sergeant showing up at the house one night in an awful state. He was throwing around all sorts of wild allegations about Jimmy, but Mum soon set him straight. 'That's what good friends are for,' she would say.

Nothing was too much trouble. Mum even wrote a letter to the Queen one day asking if Jimmy could visit Buckingham Palace. And guess what, it happened! Jimmy even got a little souvenir medal from his trip.

Sadly, Des, time moves on and neither of them is with us anymore. I miss them both dearly, but it would give me some crumb of comfort to know that they were still together in the afterlife.

Thanks in advance!

From, Mark

Jimmy loved giving hugs

Helping the kids

Jimmy and Maggie

Des Says:

Mark, your Mum sounds like she was a lovely kind woman and Jimmy was clearly nothing less than a saint. I was so emotional reading your letter that I had both tears and snot rolling down my face simultaneously.

In fact, your story touched my heart so much that I decided to use the special Des Montgomerie Celestite Meditation Crystals™ (only £180.00 plus P&P) to communicate with Maggie and Jimmy. As you know, I only use these incredibly powerful stones in very special circumstances.

For this particular ceremony, the crystals were arranged into the famous Des Montgomerie pentagram formation, I then lay in the middle of them, wearing only my Celestial Loincloth™ (£35.00 plus P&P) which allowed me comfortable and easy access to the afterlife. Details of this wonderful technique are explained in my latest book: Journey to the Other Side (£19.99 plus P&P).

Mark, you've got nothing to worry about because Maggie and Jimmy are living happily together in the burning depths of hell. They've had no trouble at all fitting in and I've even got word that a special welcoming committee was arranged upon their arrival.

I actually managed to speak directly to your Mum, and she told me that Jimmy is having a whale of a time. 'He's up to his old tricks,' she said, rolling her eyes and smiling. She's just as beautiful as ever by the way!

Apparently they've even managed to catch up with a few other old friends – a Chilean chap and an American actor called Ronald, I believe. She said they have a great three-way relationship, and sometimes Jimmy likes to join in, too. I hope these words offer you the comfort you desire.

She also wanted you to know that she's been looking up at us all and is particularly proud of what a fat albino named Alexander de Pfeffel has been doing recently. Does this mean anything to you?

I must say that I've never been more honoured to help than I was for you, Mark. Your Mum and Jimmy are absolute darlings and I think it warms all our hearts to know how much fun they are still having.

> **She's just as beautiful as ever**

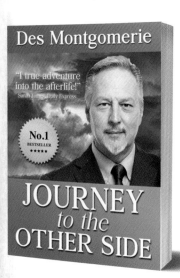

Des Montgomerie

"A true adventure into the afterlife!"
Sarah James, Daily Express

No.1 BESTSELLER
★★★★★

JOURNEY to the OTHER SIDE

Picture Credits

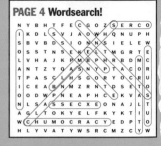

Puzzles Answers:

The publishers would like to thank the following sources for their kind permission to reproduce the pictures in this book. Key: T=top, B=bottom, L=left, R=right, C=centre.

FRONT COVER PHOTOGRAPHS: (Boris Johnson) Samir Hussein/WireImage/Getty Images; (Keir Starmer) Joel Goodman/LNP/Shutterstock; (Michael Gove) Shutterstock; (Nigel Farage) Stephen Simpson/Shutterstock; (Barnard Castle) David Taylor Photography/Alamy; (Dominic Cummings) Shutterstock; (Matt Hancock) Ben Cawthra/Shutterstock; (Jacob Rees Mogg) Facundo Arrizabalaga/EPA-EFE/Shutterstock.

ALAMY: /CBW: 58R; /Mike Ford: 47BL; /PA: 43BR; /Sputnik: 38R; /Washington Imaging: 47TC

GETTY IMAGES: /Andy Buchanan/AFP: 22TR

I-IMAGES: /Pete Maclaine: 42R

NEWS LICENCING: /Chris Eades: 43TL; /News Group Newspapers Ltd: 62BR

PA IMAGES: /David Jones: 63R

SHUTTERSTOCK: 7TR, 8B, 12BL, 29BR, 48R, 50R; /06photo: 48-49C; /1000 Words: 47TL; /ALX1618: 11BR; /ANL: 63T; /AP: 7BR, 12R, 34C, 35C; /abimages: 26C; /Action Press: 11TL, 39TL; /Bruce Adams: 10R, 43BC; /Kurit Afshen: 46TR; /Anna Aiva: 33TL, 33C; /Tolga Akmen/LNP: 37TL; /Alexstr: 30L; /Marko Aliaksandr: 12-13T; /AlohaHawaii: 4BR; /aperturesound: 7BL; /Facundo Arrizabalaga/EPA-EFE: 32TL; /astarot: 35TR; /Austral: 57T; /Auto Express: 29BR; /Rudy Bagozzi: 37BR; /Jeffrey Banks: 54R; /Matt Baron/BEI: 15BL; /BarracudaDesigns: 23BL; /David Bebber: 29T; /Bei: 39TL; /Beretta/Sims: 29T; /bestbee: 24BR; /Broadimage: 9L; /Alexander Caminada: 17TC; /Canadian Press: 26BR; /Chris Capstick: 33BR; /Kip Carroll: 22L; /Ben Cawthra: 51T; /christianrosepix: 59BR; /Stuart Clarke: 44L; /Corona Borealis Studio: 4TL; /Creatista: 12BL, 13B; /Zachary Culpin: 44TR; /Mike Daines: 57T; /Alan Davidson: 33TL, 36BR, 59BC; /Joanne Davidson: 14BL; /digitalreflections: 26BR; /design1983: 22BR; /docent: 17B; /Chris Dorney: 23R; /Maria Dryfhout: 24T; /Eskymaks: 27TR; /Alberto Estevez/EPA: 50R; /Gareth Everett/Huw Evans: 5L; /Alexey Fedorenko: 34BC; /FiledIMAGE: 56T; /Iakov Filimonov: 55TC; /Vickie Flores/EPA-EFE: 61BR; /Fotokolia: 7BR; /Viktoria Gavrilina: 27TR; /Vadim Georgiev: 62-63BKG; /Lydie Gigerichova/imageBROKER: 53BL; /glenda: 55TL; /Sergii Gnatiuk: 59TC; /Lukas Gojda: 30BR; /Joe Gough: 54BR; /Ian Grainger: 23L; /Richard Griffin: 30C; /Cliff Hands: 53TL; /David Hartley: 16, 26L, 37BC, 48R; /Dave Head: 47T; /Jiang Hongyan: 26BL; /Andy Hooper/ANL: 56-57B; /Christopher Hotton: 34-35; /Dirk Hudson: 41TR; /Kathy Hutchins: 22L; /ITV: 8R, 37TL; /irin-k: 15BL; /Hugo Jaeger/The LIFE Picture Collection: 14R; /Nigel Jarvis: 34BL; /Nils Jorgensen: 5T, 37TR, 48R; /Just dance: 21C; /kmls: 62-63BKG; /Evgeny Karandaev: 15T; /Kekyalyaynen: 54TR; /Keystone/Zuma: 38BL; /Kletr: 23TR; /Maria Kovaleva: 40BR; /Kpad: 7CL; /Volodymyr Krasyuk: 7BCR; /kryzhov: 58C; /Pelevina Ksinia: 27TR; /Pooja Kumaris: 60-61BKG; /LStockStudio: 35TL; /Keith Larby: 11T; /Tony Larkin: 28L; /Mike Lawn: 26TR; /Richard M Lee: 4L; /legenda: 20TR, 21TR; /Geraint Lewis: 52R; /Ralf Liebhold: 49C; /Natalia Lisovskaya: 30T; /Miroslav Lukic: 55BR; /Charles Wayne Lytton: 28T; /makalex69: 60C, 60BR, 61C; /Mangostar: 41R; /Pryimachuk Mariana: 21C; /Marsan: 27TL; /MaxShutter: 48-49T; /Andrew McCaren/LNP: 42L, 42BL; /Ken McKay/ITV: 6R, 24L; /Rob McMillan: 36TR; /Mcpix: 7L; /Steve Meddle: 58L, 58TR; /Mediapunch: 8B; /merrymuuu: 55BC; /Alexandros Michailidis: 52T; /Jan Mika: 30TR; /Militarist: 50BR; /Minerva Studio: 62TC, 63BL; /mjheritage: 28R; /Monrudee: 23T; /mooremedia: 60TR; /Jaroslav Moravcik: 50T; /Mr.Louis: 55TR; /Mr Nai: 35BL; /Andrew Murray: 56L; /Napa: 39B; /Denis Nata: 27TR; /Jon Naustdalslid: 45TR; /News Group: 8B; /Sergey Novikov: 60T; /nullplus: 49BR; /Oldnature_picker: 26C; /Andrii Oleksiienko: 52R; /Olinchuk: 58B; /oneinchpunch: 12R; /Bartosz Ostrowski: 53R; /Andrew Parsons: 14L; /Patrick Foto: 23L; /Pavel L Photo and Video: 10R, 24L; /Ivan Pavlisko: 27TR; /Erik Pendzich: 9L; /Nai Pisage: 21TC; /Pixel-Shot: 58TR; /Anurak Pongpatimet: 42-43; /Leigh Prather: 49T; /Mark Rademaker: 27TC; /Andy Rain/EPA-EFE: 54BL; /Simon Rawles: 53BL; /Geoffrey Robinson: 60BR; /Tim Rooke: 25L; /Murray Sanders/Daily Mail: 15C; /saurabhpbhoyar: 17TR; /Susan Schmitz: 10L; /sebastock: 59R; /Dani Simmonds: 57TR; /Sipa: 7TC, 57R; /sirtravelalot: 4T; /Solent News: 42BR, 46L; /Jenny Solomon: 17TC; /Maryna Stamatova: 13C; /Ben Stansall/AP: 4R; /Startraks: 40BL; /Alex Stemmer: 46T; /SusaImages: 46BR; /Ray Tang: 41BR, 56L; /Tashsat: 54-55; /Mark Thomas: 21C; /Alexander Tolstykh: 23BL; /Triff: 37BR; /urbanbuzz: 23C; /VH-studio: 27TR; /Iulian Valentin: 27TR; /Taras Verkhovynets: 24L, 24BR, 25BR; /James Veysey: 14L, 59TR; /Yakobchuk Viacheslav: 46L; /Viktory Viktor: 30C; /Vlad61: 23BR; /Vrvirus: 44TR; /Kirsty Wigglesworth/AP: 5BR; /Alf Wilson: 9L; /Shannon Wine: 45BR; /George Cracknell Wright/LNP: 7BCL, 17B; /Richard Young: 26TR, 43TR; /Peter Zachar: 38T; /Nikki Zalewski: 62-63BKG; /Zwiebackesser: 20R

TEESSIDE LIVE: 43C

WIKIMEDIA COMMONS: 15L, 23TL, 32B, 51R; /Emir Curt: 50R; /Ella's Bubbles: 6L; /Interactive Life Forms LLC: 51R; /Jeremy Kemp: 14BR

Every effort has been made to acknowledge correctly and contact the source and/or copyright holder of each picture. Any unintentional errors or omissions will be corrected in future editions of this book.

THIS BOOK IS A PARODY

All the articles, games, competitions, images and illustrations in this book are 100% fictional. Some of the photos have also been edited for humorous purposes. A full list of those can be found below.

Acknowledgements

The author would like to thank the following for their work on this book:

Egg2, CJH, Christoph B Mark C, Micky E and Nuggbert

This is a list of the photos that have been heavily edited for humorous purposes:

P.2 – Piers Morgan and Meghan Markle, Mark Zuckerberg; P.3 – David Cameron, Boris Johnson, Vladimir Putin; P.5 – Boris Johnson; P.6 – Tony Blair; P.8 – Piers Morgan and Meghan Markle, P.9 – Piers Morgan; P.10 – Katie Hopkins, P.12 – Mark Zuckerberg twice; P.15 – Alex Jones; P.16 – Keir Starmer; P.17 – Keir Starmer; P.21 – Rishi Sunak; P.22 – Donald Trump; P.24 – Jeremy Kyle; P.25 – Jeremy Kyle; P.26 – Andrew Neil; P.29 – Jeremy Clarkson; P.31 – Laurence Fox; P.33 – Jacob Rees-Mogg; P.37 – David Cameron caravan; P.39 – Vladimir Putin; P.41 – Matt Hancock Guinness; P.46 – David Icke; P.48 – Prince Phillip; P.50 – Nigel Farage; P.51 – Dominic Raab; P.52 – David Starkey; P.53 – David Starkey; P.58 – Mary Berry; P.61 – Captain Tom

PAGE 4 Wordsearch!

PAGE 11 Explosive Puzzle!

PAGE 14 Spot the Difference

PAGE 14 Name the Wanker:
Lee Hurst

PAGE 27 Stick it in to win!

PAGE 47 Crossword!

PAGE 51 Maze

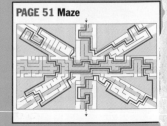